YOUR CHILD
AT PLAY

Birth to One Year

Volumes in the
Your Child at Play Series

~~~~~~~~~~~~~~~~~~~

YOUR CHILD AT PLAY:

Birth to One Year

Discovering the Senses and Learning

About the World

SECOND EDITION

MARILYN SEGAL, PH.D.

Foreword by WENDY MASI, PH.D.,
Director of the Family Center at Nova Southeastern University

NEWMARKET PRESS   NEW YORK

To my five children, who gave me first-hand experiences with the joys of motherhood.

A Mailman Family Center Book, published by Newmarket Press, drawn from research conducted at Nova Southeastern University, Ft. Lauderdale, Florida.

This book is published simultaneously in the United States of America and in Canada.

SECOND EDITION

10   9   8   7   6   5   4   3   2   1

Library of Congress Cataloging-in-Publication Data

The author gratefully acknowledges the continuing grant from the A.L. Mailman Family Foundation, Inc., which supported the writing of this book.

Segal, Marilyn M.
    Your child at play. Birth to one year / Marilyn Segal.—2nd ed.
        p.   cm.
    Includes index.
    ISBN 1-55704-334-5 (hardcover). —ISBN 1-55704-330-2 (pbk.)
    1. Play.   2. Child development.   3. Infants.   I. Title
    HQ82.S425   1998
    649'.5—DC21   97-48589
                                                        CIP

QUANTITY PURCHASES
Companies, professional groups, clubs, and other organizations may qualify for special terms when ordering quantities of this title. For information, write to Special Sales, Newmarket Press, 18 East 48th Street, New York, NY 10017; call (212) 832-3575; or fax (212) 832-3629.

Photo credits:
All photographs by Lisa Nalven Photography except for those on pages: 25, 33, 71, 75 bottom, 96, 110, 125, 148, 184, 185, 187, 203, 276, 284.

Book design by M.J. DiMassi
Manufactured in the United States of America

Acknowledgments

~~~~~~~~~~~~~~~~~~~~~~~~~~~~~~~~~~~~~

This book is a collaborative effort.

WENDY MASI, PH.D., Director of the Family Center at Nova South-eastern University, is my toughest critic. She raked through the manuscript with a fine-tooth comb and weeded out passages that were inaccurate or unclear. Dr. Masi has three delightful children of her own, who just happen to be my grandchildren.

RONI LEIDERMAN, PH.D., Director of Nova Southeastern University's Family Institute, has years of intimate experience with families of very young children. She and her staff tried out all the suggested activities with parents and babies, and helped me make appropriate changes. She identified cooperative families with adorable children to participate in our photo sessions.

ANN MCELWAIN, M.B.A., Director of Marketing and Product Development at the Family Center at Nova Southeastern University, assumed the major responsibility for implementing the photo sessions. She has an uncanny way of convincing babies to do the right thing at the right time.

SUZANNE GREGORY, my most valuable assistant, has the talent to decipher my handwriting and incorporate volumes of new material and rewrites into a manageable manuscript.

DON ADCOCK, PH.D., was the co-author of the first edition of *Your Child at Play*. He authored many of the passages that have been taken directly from the first edition.

~~~~~~

Foreword

~~~~~~

Your Child at Play is a series of books about the joy of playing with your child. When you and your child play together, you are enhancing your child's creativity and imagination, and encouraging flexible thinking. You are also getting back in touch with your own childhood, discovering a playful part of yourself that may have been buried through the years. But most important, you're connecting with your child. You are creating a bond of intimacy that will keep you and your child together in spirit, even through the often stormy teenage years.

The author of this series, Marilyn Segal, is an expert in child development, a noted professor, author, lecturer, researcher, and the founder of Nova Southeastern University's Family Center in Ft. Lauderdale, Florida, devoted to strengthening the family and enhancing the ability of parents and caregivers to nurture children. She is also a mother and grandmother whose heart and soul is invested in children, and believes more than anything in the power of play. Her home is filled with blocks, trains, books, crafts, and dolls, carefully selected so that they will be loved by all her children. Her grandchildren spend hours playing with her dollhouse and Brio set, weaving magical special worlds to which only they and their Nana are privy.

This book series is special because their author is special. She is a five foot, ninety pound powerhouse, who believes that everyone should experience the joy of play, and that playing together is at the heart of every relationship. She is my mother, my mentor, my friend. Her simple message "play together, grow together" is as powerful as it is succinct. Enjoy the books, follow your heart, and you will all have fun.

—Wendi Masi, Ph.D., Director of the Family Center
at Nova Southeastern University

~~~~

Contents

First Thoughts

~~~~~~

For new parents and even experienced parents, the first year of a baby's life is full of promise and excitement. Changes take place at such a rapid rate that getting to know your baby is filled with joy and almost daily challenges. When your baby is five or six months old you will look incredulously at a newborn baby and think, "Was my baby ever that little?"

Your Child at Play: Birth to One Year is written for parents and caregivers who want to keep in close touch with their babies during the first twelve months. Organized on a month-by-month basis, it describes subtle developmental events so you can become better observers of your own baby's developments. At the same time it provides you with a wide selection of games and activities that you can enjoy with your baby.

Begin your reading of *Your Child at Play: Birth to One Year* by selecting the section that matches your child's developmental stage. (If your baby was premature or seems to be developing at a slower pace, select a chapter that is one or two months younger than her chronological age.) Once you have found your starting point read the first section of the chapter. This section begins with "Baby's Viewpoint," and presents a general overview of your baby's developmental status. The subsections that follow—Motor Skills; Seeing, Hearing, and Feeling; and Knowing Your Baby—focus on the developmental changes that you can expect during the month.

As you read through the first section don't expect that your baby will always follow the developmental course that we outline. Babies are quite different from each other and not ever completely predictable. For many babies development takes place at an uneven pace. At times your baby appears to be at a standstill. At other times your baby will forge ahead at an astonishing pace. Babies also have different areas of strength or leading skills which serve as their cutting edge of development. For some babies this leading skill is physical, and the first indication of a developmental spurt is the achievement of a motor milestone. For other babies the developmental spurt may be marked by a new awareness of the properties of objects, or a new ability to communicate wants and needs.

The second section of each chapter is devoted to suggested activities. As you select the activities that you and your baby might enjoy, keep in mind the following points:

1. Introduce playtime activities when your baby is happy and rested. Read your baby's cues and stop playtime when she has had enough.
2. Let your baby guide your choice of activities. What does he like to do and what skills is he trying to master?
3. Feel comfortable about changing activities to make them appropriate for you and your baby. The activities we describe are just suggestions. Use your own creativity and knowledge of your baby to improve on our ideas.
4. Recognize your baby's lead skill. Provide some activities that capitalize on your baby's developmental strengths and some activities that provide practice in areas where your baby is less advanced.
5. Remember that each baby has her own threshold for stimulation. While some babies thrive on intense stimulation, other babies do better with a more subdued approach.
6. As you provide your baby with learning opportunities, remember that the most important outcome of every activity is the reinforcement of a warm and loving relationship between you and your infant.

7. Make your baby a family affair. You will discover very soon that every member of your family has his or her own style of playing. It is good for your baby to experience these differences. And while every member of the family has something special to contribute to your baby, your baby gives something special to each member of the family.

CHAPTER 1

THE NEWBORN
(BIRTH—ONE MONTH)

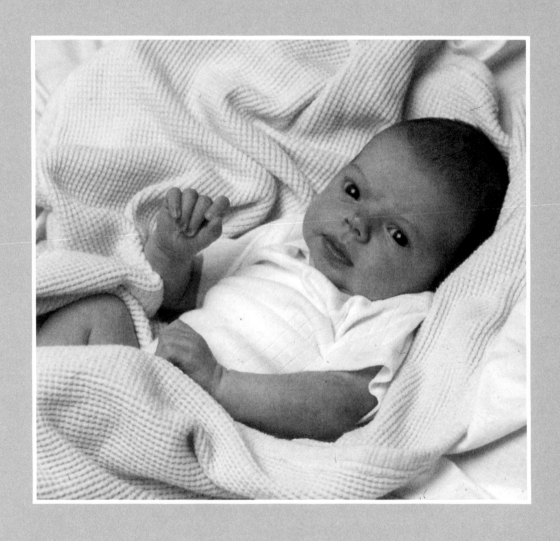

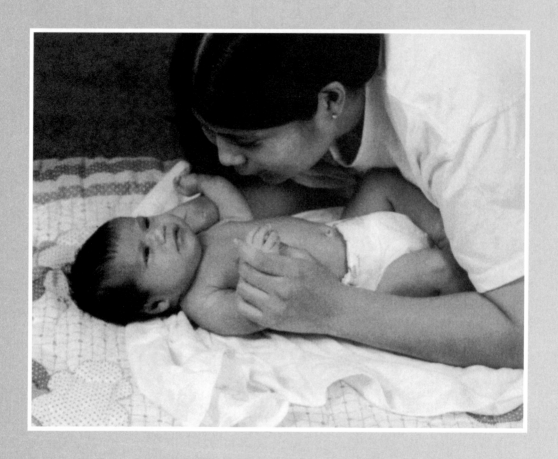

Baby's Viewpoint

Your baby is born with amazing capabilities. She gazes into your eyes, listens to your voice, and quiets when you hold her. She recognizes your voice and prefers it to all other voices. She makes connections between her own crying and your response. As you come to her crib, she anticipates feelings of comfort. Slowly, over time and on an intuitive level, she develops a sense of trust, knowing that you are there and her needs will be met. As a parent you respond to your baby's growing trust with increased confidence in yourself. You become aware of her preferences, sensitive to her pace, and supportive of her needs. In every sense of the word you become the most reliable authority on the needs and personality of your baby.

During these first days and weeks of infancy you and your baby become intertwined in a love relationship. This ever-strengthening bond is your baby's first lesson in loving. It is the prototype for other love relationships throughout your baby's life, and the source of energy for all she will ever learn.

MOTOR SKILLS

Your newborn baby is unable to feed herself or move about, but she is far from helpless. She comes into the world with an impressive set of built-in reflex behaviors. For the most part these built-in reflexes are the key to your baby's survival. When we stroke a newborn baby's cheek, her head turns and she gropes for the nipple. When a nipple is placed in her mouth, she automatically sucks and swallows. Another set of reflexes protects your baby against physical harm. When the baby's nose and mouth are covered, she turns her head to the side. When an object moves in toward her face, she automatically blinks her eyes.

Some reflexes that are present in a newborn have no direct tie to survival but do provide information about the baby's developmental status. During a postnatal checkup the pediatrician may hold the baby in different positions, make a sudden loud sound, or pass his finger along the side of the baby's foot. As the baby reacts to these and other manipulations, the pediatrician is assured that the newborn's reflexes are normal and her nervous system is intact.

While most of the reflexes that are present in the newborn disappear during the first year of life, some reflexes serve as the basis of learned behavior. Sucking begins as a reflexive behavior, but as the baby gains experience she learns to alter her sucking technique according to what she is sucking. The same is true of the grasp reflex. A newborn baby will close her hand in the same way no matter what kind of object is placed in her palm. By the age of four months, her grasp will come under voluntary control. She will focus on an object and then reach out and grasp it.

Although we tend to think of all the new babies as starting from the same point, newborns are noticeably different in their level of motor development. Some new babies are remarkably inactive. Placed on their stomach or back, they remain almost motionless until they are picked up and moved. Other babies are relatively active. Placed face down in the crib, they inch up to the top of the crib and wedge themselves in a corner. Some very active babies flip reflexively from stomach to back.

A second dimension of difference in new babies is their degree of muscle tone. Some babies appear to be especially tight, with knees pulled up, arms close to their bodies, and hands held tightly in a fist. Other babies are more floppy, with less tone in their limbs.

A third difference among new babies is their reaction to stimulation. Some babies appear to be easily upset. A slight noise can jerk their whole being, and their limbs flail out of control. Sometimes, for no apparent reason, a shiver travels through their bodies. Other babies find ways to self-comfort, even in the first year of life. They have learned how to get their hands in or near their mouths and they use the hand-mouth position as a way of quieting down. When these babies kick their feet there is a rhythm and pattern to their movements.

While differences in activity level, muscle tone, and the ability to self-comfort may reflect neurological maturity, some of these differences are associated with biologically based temperament. There is general agreement among experts that temperamental differences can be described as the clustering of characteristics that have physical and emotional manifestations. Some babies are described by their parents as easy. These babies are generally happy, alert, interested in new experiences, with regular sleeping and eating patterns. Other babies are described by their parents as fussy. These babies are likely to be irritable, difficult to soothe, easily overstimulated, with irregular sleeping and eating patterns. Still other babies are described by their parents as laid back. These babies are likely to be relatively inactive, difficult to arouse, and somewhat wary of new experiences. While many temperamental characteristics change as the baby matures, differences in temperament can persist through childhood.

SEEING, HEARING, AND FEELING

Your baby enters the world with a built-in repertoire of adaptive skills. She blinks her eyes when a bright light is turned on or when an object comes toward her face. She tracks a moving target, such as an approaching face, for a short distance.

Another striking characteristic of young infants is their ability to recognize differences in smell, taste, and texture. When presented with two nursing pads, infants will turn toward the pad that belonged to their mother. They accept a drop of sweet water and reject water that tastes salty, bitter, or sour. They recognize differences in texture and will respond to different tactile stimulation in different ways. Brisk rubbing with a towel alerts a baby, while a gentle massage will put her to sleep.

Your baby's reactions to stimulation depend not only on the kind of stimulation she is offered, but also on her "state of arousal." Experts in infant development point out that babies have different states of arousal or different ways of being asleep and awake. The baby who is awake may be quiet, alert, actively kicking and flailing, or crying.

Your baby is also born with an innate capacity to use her senses to take in new information. Interestingly enough, she even shows visual preferences. She seeks out designs with a distinct focal point, and is particularly attracted to moving objects and to black and white configurations. Think about the characteristics of human eyes. It's hard to escape the conclusion that the baby is uniquely programmed to make early eye contact with her parents.

We now know that in addition to innate visual skills, the newborn baby has remarkable auditory capabilities. Not only are we certain that a

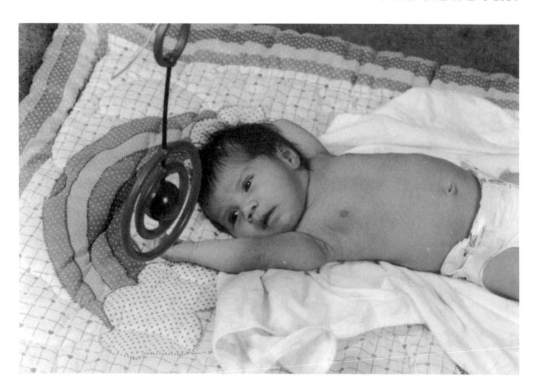

baby hears from the moment of birth, we also recognize that babies still in the womb react to sound. The newborn will turn her head toward the source of sound, alert to a sound that is new, and tune out sounds that are repetitive, loud, or steady. Even more striking is the fact that the baby can discriminate between a human voice and any other sound. In other words, just as the baby is uniquely programmed to look into your eyes, she also has a built-in tendency to listen to your voice.

While the infant's ability to discriminate between different sounds and different images is well documented, there is also convincing evidence that babies are born with the capacity to coordinate hearing, seeing, and feeling. When your newborn hears the tinkle of a rattle, she will search for it with her eyes. She will also look at her hand when you are stroking it. Your baby's ability to make associations between feeling, hearing, and being touched continues to develop during the first months.

The way your newborn responds to events in the environment is very much determined by her state of arousal. A baby who is in a quiet alert state may respond to the tinkle of a bell by a momentary cessation of activity followed by a visible effort to turn toward the source of sound. The same baby in an active or crying state may ignore the bell completely.

KNOWING YOUR BABY

The newborn period is a time of adjustment for both you and your infant. Parents need to adjust their routine in response to their baby's needs. The baby must adapt both physiologically and psychologically to life outside the womb. An important part of a baby's adjustment is self regulation. She is learning to regulate her state of arousal so that she can move smoothly from a sleep state to a state of quiet alertness, or from an awake state to a state of quiet sleep. Much of your energy as a parent in these early weeks will be devoted to helping your baby make these transitions.

Infants differ in the amount of time they are in a state of quiet alertness. Some babies are alert and attentive when they first awaken from sleep, while other infants wake up hungry and need to be nursed right away. Some babies are quiet and alert once they have been fed, while nursing makes other babies drowsy.

Reaching a state of quiet alertness is important for a newborn. When your infant is in a state of quiet alertness she looks around, attends to sounds, and appears wide-eyed and aware. Her energies are directed to taking in information, providing you with a special opportunity to stimulate her and to communicate with her.

If your infant spends very little time awake and attentive, you can help her. When she awakens hungry, give her a moment or so to look around before you begin nursing. When she finishes nursing, hold her and talk to her before she falls asleep. After a while your infant will spend more time in the quiet alert state, listening to your voice and looking around.

Whether your baby quite naturally achieves a state of quiet alertness or needs some help, you have to be careful not to overdo. Too much stimulation can be stressful for even the most placid infant. Be sensitive to her cues. If she purses her lips, tightens her fists, curls her toes, or gets fussy and turns away, she is signaling her need for a rest.

In general, the most difficult state for a newborn to modulate without help is crying. Although babies differ in the amount and kind of soothing they need when they are distressed, all babies need some calming on at least a daily basis.

Some babies quiet if they are held securely in their parents' arms or wrapped in a soft blanket. Other babies are upset by any kind of restraint, and quiet more easily if they are placed on a flat surface with no covers or swaddling. Most babies are comforted by movement, but the kind of movement that is most comforting is different for different babies. Which of the following kinds of movements works best with your baby?

- Walking around the room with your baby held up to your shoulder.
- Holding your baby over your shoulder, or against your shoulder, as you rock from side to side.
- Swaddling your baby in a sheet or light blanket.

- Holding your baby against your shoulder and patting her rhythmically on the back.
- Holding your baby across your knees, moving your knees up and down or back and forth, or patting your baby gently on the buttocks.
- Rocking very slowly in a rocking chair with your baby prone across your knees or upright against your shoulder.
- Fast, rhythmic rocking in a rocking chair.
- Placing your baby in a carriage which you push back and forth.
- Taking your baby for a walk in a carriage, a backpack, or a front sling.
- Placing your baby in a hammock and swinging it gently back and forth.
- Taking your baby for a ride in the car.

Sounds as well as movements are soothing for a baby, but here again babies have their own preferences. Some babies quiet best to a steady sound, such as a clock ticking, a simulated heart beat, or the whirr of a washing machine. Other babies react best to low-pitched talking, monotonous chanting, or quiet whispering. Still other babies prefer music: a lullaby, a music box, or classical music. When all else fails and your baby continues to cry, you may want to put her in a quiet room and let her cry for a few minutes. With some babies crying is an outlet for tension. After a short bout of crying, she will be ready to settle down.

We have talked so far about how sensitive and loving parents help their infant make her first accommodations to life outside the womb.

But just as your baby is supported by you, you are supported by your baby. When your baby alerts to the sound of your voice or quiets to your touch, she is letting you know without words how important you are to each other.

Infants have two major means of communication: smiling and crying. Both follow a similar progression. In the first weeks, they are spontaneous; that is, the baby is responding to internal physiological stimulation. Crying reflects internal discomfort or pain; smiling results from a sudden drop in the discharge level of the nervous system. Gradually the balance shifts. Crying and smiling are increasingly controlled by external events, and as a result the baby begins to communicate directly with her parents.

The development of the smile during the first month or two is particularly interesting. Initially fleeting smiles occur during sleep. Then by the second week your baby may smile with her eyes open, usually after feeding. This smile is accompanied by a kind of glassy, faraway look. By the third or fourth week a qualitative change takes place. The infant attends to her parent's high-pitched voice, eye-to-eye contact is established, and her parent is rewarded with a truly social smile.

A baby who is happy and responsive most of the time inspires confidence in her parents, and gets the family off to a good start. A restless and irritable baby who is not easily soothed by the nurturant behaviors of her parents presents a greater challenge. First-time parents are likely to interpret their baby's irritability as a sign of their own inadequacy. Once they recognize that the baby's fussiness is physiologically based, they regain their self-confidence and are able to manage these difficult first weeks. Through trial and error, parents find special ways of quieting their baby—perhaps swaddling or vigorous rocking, or perhaps just allowing the baby to cry for a while until she falls asleep. Most important, they realize that their baby's difficulty with self-regulation does not indicate a long-term personality characteristic.

Whether or not their baby has settled down, new parents may continue to experience negative emotions. The young mother, perhaps suffering from postpartum blues—or exhaustion as a result of sleepless nights—may find herself sliding into a depression, or getting snappish with other members of the family. The father, despite his proud smile, may sometimes feel that the baby is taking away not only a portion of his freedom, but also a portion of his wife's concern. Over time, these tensions will fade. Babies sleep for longer periods, parents are less exhausted, and they gradually become accustomed to sharing each other with their baby. Parents gain new confidence in their ability to parent and the stage is set for a mutually rewarding relationship between you and your baby.

Suggested Activities

AN INTRODUCTION

In the first month, the most important task that your baby has to accomplish is adjustment to life outside the womb. Much of the time your baby will be asleep. During her waking hours, she will be tuned into her physiological needs. Periods of quiet alertness, when your baby is ready to take in new information, are sparse and short-lived. This means that you should not plan on a special play period for a newborn baby. Simply take advantage of spontaneous opportunities. These opportunities are most likely to arise when your baby is fed and contented. Remember that babies have different thresholds for stimulation, and if you overstimulate your baby you may change her state from quiet alertness to fussiness or crying.

SETTING THE STAGE

Just Enough Handling

Your baby needs and loves to be handled. Judge how much holding your baby enjoys. Some babies get tense and irritable from too much han-

dling. Others become listless and unresponsive if they are not held or handled. Read your own baby. Is she fussier or less fussy when she is carried around? Does she enjoy being in an infant carrier? Does she prefer an infant carrier in which she faces her parents, or one that faces her outward and allows her to look around?

Baby's Positions

Place your baby in different positions when she is awake. Sometimes she can be on her stomach, sometimes on her back, sometimes on her side. Pediatricians often suggest turning a newborn on her back as soon as she falls asleep. There is some evidence that sleeping stomach down could be associated with "Sudden Infant Death Syndrome."

Baby Diary

Instead of a calendar, keep a pencil and pad in your baby's room. You will want to record the interesting things your baby is doing.

Happy Times

Smile and laugh with your baby. A baby seems to be able to tell when you are having fun with her.

On the Double

Respond quickly to your baby's needs. If you give a baby appropriate attention when she needs it, she is less likely to ask for attention when she doesn't need it. Remember, you cannot spoil an infant.

Playing it Safe

Take your baby home from the hospital in a safety-approved car seat, in the back seat of the car.

Photo Album

Take photos of your baby and the family on a regular basis. When your baby is older, she will love seeing herself as a baby.

Journal

Begin a journal of your feelings as you begin the parenting journey. Share your thoughts, your joys, and your challenges in a journal that can be continued and cherished in the years to come.

SEEING, HEARING, AND FEELING

Musical Mobile

During moments when your baby is quiet and awake she will catch sight of a mobile and her eyes will follow its movements. This will awaken her interest in the world outside her crib (around her, outside herself). Musical mobiles are especially attractive to young infants.

Penlight

Cover a penlight with red or yellow cellophane. While your baby is on her back, move the light slowly from side to side. At first your baby will look at it just for a second, but after a while she will follow it with her eyes.

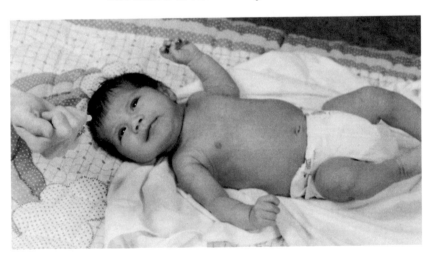

Early Imitation

Stick out your tongue! Some two- and three-week-old infants can imitate you when you stick out your tongue. Give it a try!

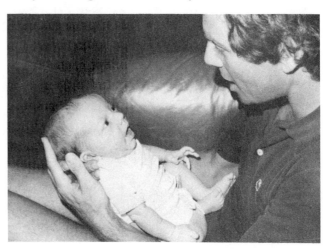

Wind Chime

Hang a wind chime in a place where your baby can watch it move and listen to the sound. This will give her an opportunity to associate a pleasant sight with a pleasant sound. If the chime is over the crib, your baby is likely to watch it for a few minutes and then drop off to sleep.

Dancing to Music

Your newborn will enjoy the familiar rocking movements she has felt for so many months in the womb. Listen to music as you hold and gently dance with your baby.

Rattle Shake

Shake a rattle first on one side of the baby's head, then on the other. Begin by shaking it slowly—then vigorously. After a while, your baby will realize that the sound she hears comes from somewhere outside herself. She will search with her eyes for the thing that is making the sound. If your baby shows signs of distress or begins to tune out, shake the rattle less vigorously or find a quieter rattle.

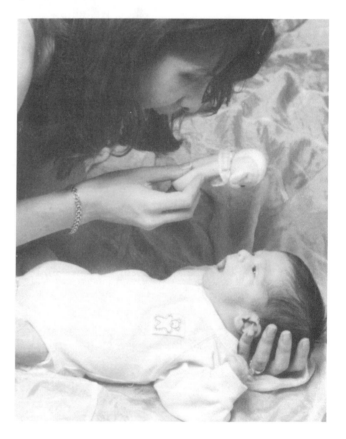

Tight Hold

Place your own finger or a rattle in the palm of your baby's hand. Your baby will tighten her fingers around it.

Exercising

Kicking Practice

Place your baby on a firm mat (a crib mattress or playpen mat is fine) without any covers. Give your baby a few minutes to kick her feet and move her arms. If she begins to cry, try to calm her. If she is still agitated, try again another day.

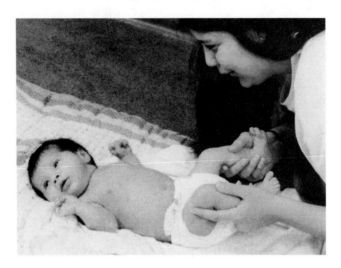

DAILY ROUTINES

Mealtime

Happy Mealtime

Whether you breast-feed or bottle feed your baby, feeding time should be happy and relaxing for both baby and you. And remember, your baby knows better than you when she has had enough to eat, so don't push her to have a little more. Enjoy the special moments shared during feedings. Tension is catching and so is confidence.

Touch Time

As your baby is feeding, gently massage her head, fingers, and shoulders. Your baby will associate her feeding with your loving touch. Some babies enjoy listening to singing while they suck. Other babies will listen to their mother's voice and forget to suck. If your baby is easily distracted, reserve your singing for burp time or pause time. Whether you breast or bottle feed, your baby will enjoy the feeling of her skin in contact with your skin. At times, keep your baby in just a diaper during feeding.

Bathtime

Beginning Bath

Bathe your baby in a baby bathtub. (Check with your doctor before giving your baby her first bath.) Talk or sing softly as you wash your baby, rubbing gently with a soft washcloth. Place a towel on the bottom of the tub if your baby is squirmy and needs a softer cushion.

Communicating Through Touch

After her bath, your baby is ready to be massaged. Using baby oil or a cold-pressed vegetable oil, gently massage her arms, hands, legs, feet, back, tummy, and buttocks. Use firm, broad,

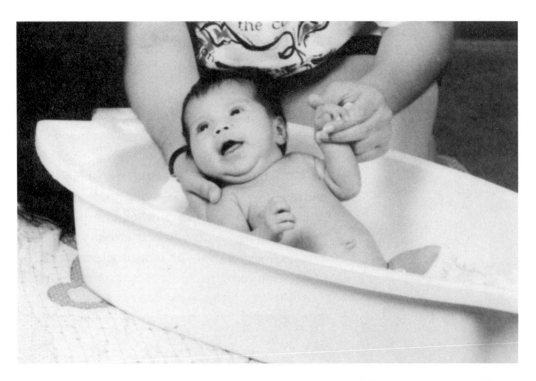

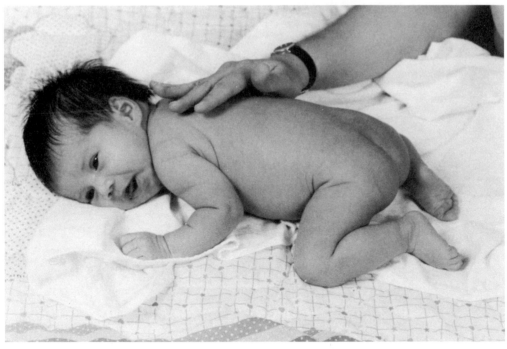

circular strokes. Continue only as long as your baby is quiet and content.

Diapering/Dressing

Tummy Kisses

As you change your baby's diapers, gently kiss her tummy, toes, and fingers. This gentle stimulation helps her develop an early awareness of her body parts. Not only is your baby becoming aware of herself but she is also feeling your expression of love.

Dressing Down

Don't overdress your baby. If your room is between 70° and 75°, your baby will be quite comfortable in a shirt and diaper. Babies get hot, "rashy," and uncomfortable when they are overdressed.

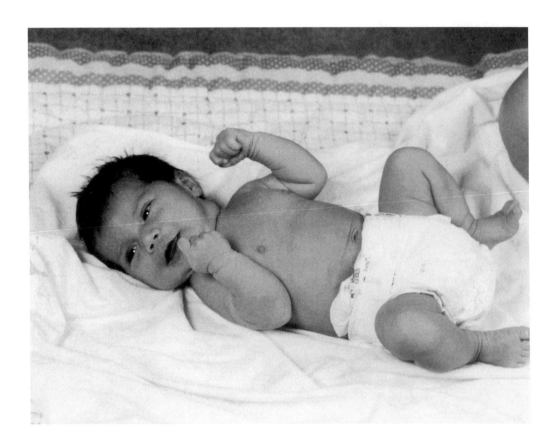

A Family Affair

Both you and your spouse should participate in diapering, feeding, and dressing the baby. Daily routines provide a special opportunity for parents to bond with their baby.

Quiet Time

Music Time

Play a radio or wind up a music box when you place your baby in her crib. Quiet music helps to soothe your baby.

Audiotaping

As an alternative to the expensive Teddy Bear toy with taped sounds of the uterus, try taping your dishwasher or washing machine. The whooshing sounds played back for your baby help to soothe and comfort her.

Musical Toy

Put a soft musical toy in your baby's crib when she is falling asleep. She will become accustomed to the sound and associate it with sleep time. When she is a few months older, placing the wind-up toy in her crib will help her fall asleep.

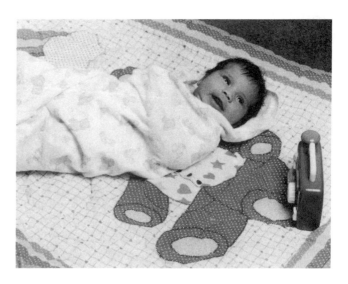

Pacifier

Many parents find that a pacifier calms their baby and helps her fall asleep. If your baby resists a pacifier, you may have to hold it in her mouth for a few seconds until she gets used to it. If she is still resistant, try a different type of pacifier. Often infants will reject one type of pacifier and accept a different type. When your baby is learning to use a pacifier, give it to her when she is quiet and content. When babies are agitated or distressed, they are not likely to learn a new skill.

Stroller Walk

Weather permitting, take your baby for a stroller ride. The steady movement will help her fall asleep.

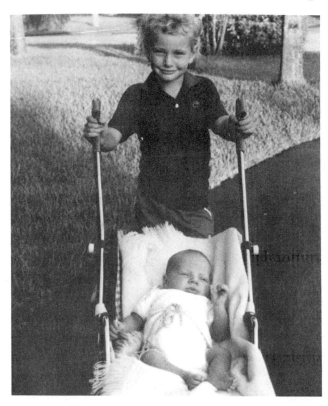

CHAPTER 2

ONE MONTH

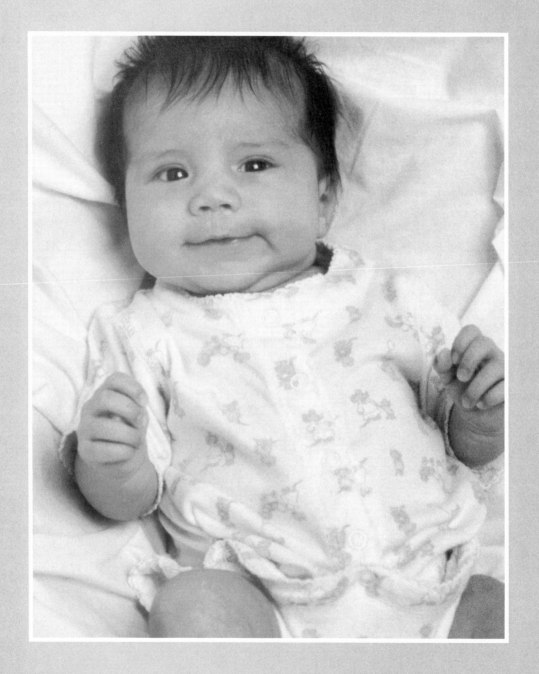

Baby's Viewpoint

In the newborn chapter, we talked about the beginning of a communication system between parent and child. During the second month of life, you will see this system developing as your baby becomes increasingly responsive to parent-child exchanges. At the same time, you will watch your baby develop greater muscle control and an expanded capacity to respond to the sights and sounds he experiences.

You will become more aware of your baby's unique personality as he increases his capacity to take in and respond to new information. At one month, you can already identify characteristics that make your baby special. "Cooing" conversation with your baby helps you become attuned to his natural rhythm, and you will recognize when to provide more stimulation and when to turn away. You learn new ways of handling your baby during bouts of irritability. You discover techniques to help him maintain a state of quiet alertness, or settle down to sleep.

One of the ways that you can help your baby learn to quiet himself is to teach him how to suck a pacifier. Some babies suck a pacifier automatically, but others will reject it forcefully at first. Encourage your baby to use his pacifier when he is calm and well fed. If your baby resists or spits out a pacifier, be gentle but persistent. Hold the pacifier in your baby's mouth while you rock him and sing to him. Buy two or three different kinds of pacifiers so that you can discover the one that is easiest for him to suck. After a while your efforts will pay off and your baby will use the pacifier as a way of calming himself down and putting himself to sleep. The pacifier is a tool that both you and your baby will appreciate in the months ahead.

MOTOR SKILLS

Your one-month-old is gaining control of his body. He has lost some of his jerky, spasmodic movements, and is beginning to move his arms and legs in a smooth and rhythmic pattern. The tremors and startles that are so characteristic of the newborn are beginning to disappear.

One of the most noticeable changes is your baby's increased head control. When placed on his stomach in the crib, he can move his head effortlessly from side to side. Especially strong babies may even lift their heads off the sheet and look around the crib. This increased head control is also evident when your baby is held on your shoulder. However, no matter how strong your baby is, head control is far from perfect. Make sure to cradle his head in your arms when you lift him out of the crib or carry him around the room.

Although month-old babies do not usually move around, occasionally we will find an active month-old who wiggles up to a corner of his crib, or even turns from stomach to back. Even inactive babies may be capable of sudden movement. To be on the safe side, it's better not to leave even the tiniest baby by himself on a raised surface such as a changing table or bed.

In addition to an improvement in head control, the one-month-old baby has become much more adept at waving his arms and kicking his legs. Not only can he exercise his arms and legs in a smooth, rhythmic pattern, but he can speed up or slow down his movement in rhythm with a human voice. When you speak to your baby in a slow, steady rhythm, his arm and leg movements are slow and steady. Try speaking faster and with more excitement and watch how his kicking speeds up.

SEEING, HEARING, AND FEELING

When we talked about the newborn baby, we talked about states of arousal. We said that babies have different ways of being in the world, different ways of being asleep, and different ways of being awake. In the month-old baby, these states are more discrete. It is easy to tell when your baby is in a quiet or an active sleep, and when your baby is in a quiet alert state rather than an awake active state.

In the quiet alert state, a one-month-old baby can follow a moving object with his eyes. He focuses with interest on an object or a picture that is eight to twelve inches in front of him. If the object is especially interesting the baby might even "coo" at it. Then after a few minutes he looks away. This is called "habituation." It is as if he is saying, "Yes, I know that object now." If you change the object that is in front of your baby, or introduce a second object, his visual exploration begins again. This helps explain why mobiles, with changing objects or patterns, are of particular interest to your baby.

The one-month-old baby is interested in new sounds as well as new sights. He can tell the difference between talking and other sounds, and shows a definite preference for listening to a voice. When first presented with a new sound, your baby "alerts"; that is, he stops moving his arms and legs and appears to be listening to the sound. After two or three presentations of the same sound, your baby habituates and does not attend to the sound. If you change the sound, such as changing from a bell to a squeak toy or a rattle, your baby will attend to the new presentation.

At one month old, your baby is getting better at associating the things he hears and the things he sees. With a little practice he will be able to look up at his bell as soon as he hears its tinkle. A baby reacts differently to different kinds of sounds. Music quiets him, a loud noise startles him, a high pitched whistle or an interesting jingle will hold his attention.

KNOWING YOUR BABY

From the moment of birth, babies are distinct individuals, differing from one another in many important ways. By the time your baby is one month old, you will begin to really know him. You can describe your baby on a continuum from quiet to restless, from contented to irritable, from active to slow moving, from easy to soothe to difficult to soothe, from predictable to erratic, from quick to respond to slow to respond. You know how your baby likes to be held and the position that works best for putting him to sleep. You can identify his pain cry, his hunger cry, and the cry that means, "There is nothing really wrong. I just want some cuddling." It is important to pay attention to all his cries now. Babies who are attended to promptly and consistently learn to trust and tend to cry less in the months ahead.

Your one-month-old baby has lost his sleepy newborn look. He stays awake for longer periods of time before and after feedings, but he still is not ready for too much stimulation. When your baby is exposed to too much noise, too much light, or too much jostling, he cannot sort out all of the separate sensations. Overwhelmed by it all, he reacts with irritability. In fact, many one-month-olds have a particular time of the day when they are prone to become overtired and fussy. During this period of restlessness, some babies respond to cuddling, rocking, or rhythmic patting on the backside. Others will stop their crying and go to sleep if they are wrapped in a blanket or tucked snuggly in a bassinet. This may be a good time to offer your baby his pacifier, if he is comforted by it.

A very active or restless baby, however, may not respond to any of these techniques, and his high-pitched insistent crying creates tensions in the household. This hard-to-soothe baby may need to release built-up tensions with a short period of crying. The following procedure works well for parents with a hard-to-soothe baby.

1. Complete bedtime routines such as feeding, diapering, bathing, and massaging at a relaxed and steady pace.

2. Sit in a rocking chair in a semi-darkened room. Hold your baby over your shoulder while you rock gently back and forth, singing a tune. (If your baby tenses up in the over-the-shoulder position, place him on his stomach across your knees or put him in a large comfortable carriage that can be shaken gently). Chant to your baby in a low, steady voice.

3. After five minutes of rocking, listen to the sound of his cry. Is he beginning to settle down? Is the cry less piercing and intense? If you feel that the cry is beginning to sound sleepier and less urgent, continue to rock for another five minutes.

4. Perhaps your baby's cry has maintained or regained its frantic quality. If this happens, try placing your baby gently on his side or back in the crib. Turn on a soft radio or music box and tiptoe out of the room.

5. If the crying continues for more than ten minutes, go through the routine again. Make sure that your pace is consistent, calm, quiet, and self-assured.

6. Finally, if your baby continues to have problems settling down, check with your pediatrician.

Although at one month your baby is not ready to face a crowd, he is likely to enjoy social interaction. Play a "face to face" game with your baby. Let your baby look at you, look away, then look at you again. In this familiar routine, you and your baby are practicing a kind of turn-taking routine which is the first step in language learning. After a while your baby will begin to make cooing noises. Although his repertoire of sounds may be limited to one or two front vowel sounds, in a very real sense he is learning how to converse.

It is fun to watch a parent engaging in a conversation with his month-old baby. The parent may raise his eyebrows, open his eyes wide, and round his mouth. Or he may knit his brow, squint his eyes, and purse his lips. He may nod his head and move in closer to the baby's face, or withdraw it slightly and turn to the side. During these unconscious antics, the parent is modeling the non-verbal components of our language system for the baby. For example, an open expression, with face fully presented, signals a desire to interact. It is an invitation for the baby to respond. A more closed expression, with face averted, signals a temporary pause in the conversation. The parent recognizes that his baby is momentarily uncomfortable and wants a short break.

These early conversations, as brief as they are, follow a predictable course. At first the parent's voice is high pitched in order to capture the baby's attention. As baby responds with "ahs" and "ohs," the parent becomes more animated, and the baby reaches a crescendo of excitement. As the baby's excitement subsides, the parent's voice lowers and he looks away. In a few seconds parent and baby face each other again and a new exchange begins. As parent and baby practice these back and forth conversations, they establish a smooth, enjoyable routine.

Suggested Activities

Your one-month-old is ready for some play time. You can introduce play activities when your baby is quiet and alert, or when you are changing his diaper or giving him a bath. Keep your play time brief. In the next few months, your baby will become increasingly alert and interactive, and will enjoy these same activities for longer stretches of time.

SETTING THE STAGE

Baby Talk

A baby's favorite sound is a human voice. Greet your baby as you come into the room and talk to him whenever you are together, telling him what you are doing. Use a high-pitched voice when you want to get your baby's attention, and a low-pitched voice when you want to soothe your baby. Changing from high pitch to lower pitch and back again to high pitch is a way of maintaining attention.

Father Play

Father play is different from mother play. Because each parent brings his baby a different kind of stimulation, it is important for parents to share the routine care of babies.

Changing the Scene

Place your baby in different positions so that he can look at different things. When taking your baby on an automobile ride, for example, place a bright pattern over the car seat to make his view exciting. (Make sure your baby is in a safety-approved car seat whenever you are in the car). Hang brightly colored pictures above the changing table. Your baby spends quite a bit of time glancing at the ceiling while being changed, and will enjoy looking at the colors and shapes.

SEEING, LISTENING, AND FEELING

Tracking Fun

Let your baby follow a rattle, a flashlight, or a brightly colored toy with his eyes. With the object 10 to 12 inches away from baby, move the object from left to right. When your baby can follow it across the midline, introduce up-and-down tracking from baby's hairline to his chin. Finally, experiment with a circular movement. Remember to be sensitive to your baby and stop playing when he has had enough or seems frustrated.

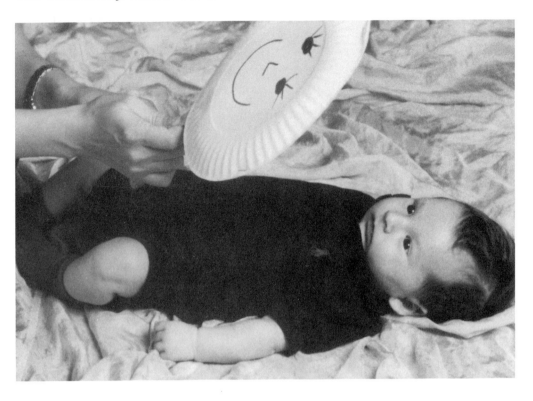

Plate Puppet

Make a simple plate puppet by drawing a face on a paper plate and pasting on a cardboard handle. Move the plate puppet in and out and back and forth about ten inches from your baby's eyes. After awhile your baby will not only follow the plate puppet with his eyes, but will greet it with a smile.

Look at Me

Let your baby track your face. As you move from left to right, your baby will follow you with his eyes and turn his head.

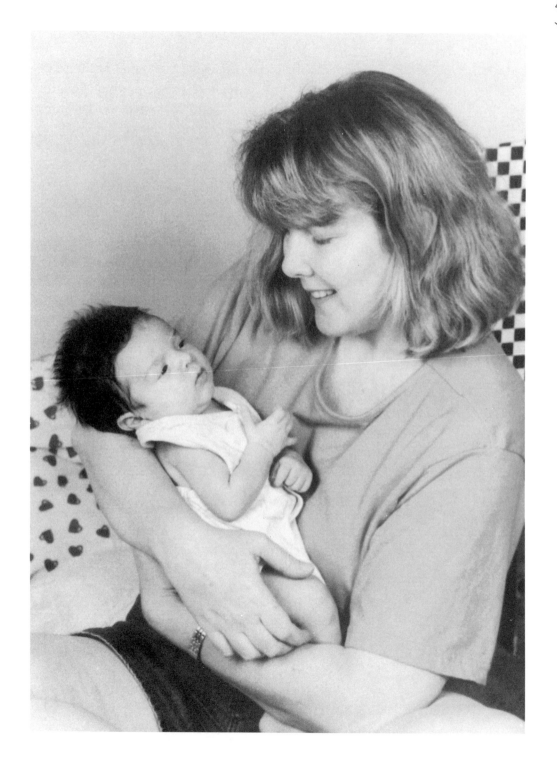

Bouncing Pet

Attach a piece of elastic to a small stuffed animal. Attach the elastic to the ceiling. Position your baby under it and make the animal jump and bounce. In later months, your baby will try to catch and grasp it.

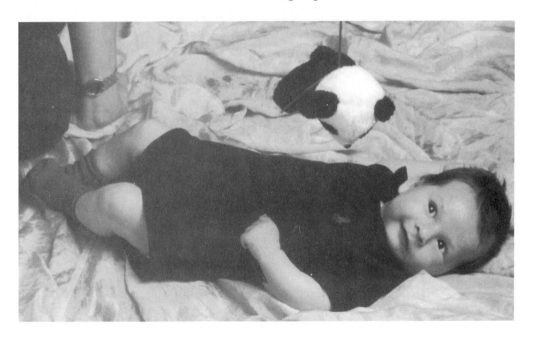

See-Through Crib Bumpers

Using clear plastic crib bumpers lets your baby see outside the crib.

Mobile Watch

Hang a mobile over your baby's crib. As you select a mobile, think of how the mobile looks from the baby's point of view. Place it on one side for a few days and then change it to the other side. When you feel that your baby can

focus on the mobile for a few moments, place a mobile on each side of the crib. After a while your baby will shift his gaze from one mobile to the other.

Nursery Rhyme Time

Introduce your baby to the rhythm and cadence of a nursery rhyme. Use old favorites like "Rock-A-Bye-Baby," "One, Two, Buckle My Shoe," and "Where is Thumbkin?," or make up your own. Take a familiar tune and simply change the words. This jingle goes to "Frère Jacque":

Hello Baby, Hello Baby,
How are you? How are you?
Oh! I love you so much,
Oh! I love you so much,
Yes I do . . .
Yes I do.

Where Am I

Talk to your baby from different places in the room. As he looks for you, he is beginning to co-ordinate sight and sound.

Finger and Toe Rub

Rub his fingers and toes one at a time. Your baby will enjoy the sensation and it will increase his body awareness.

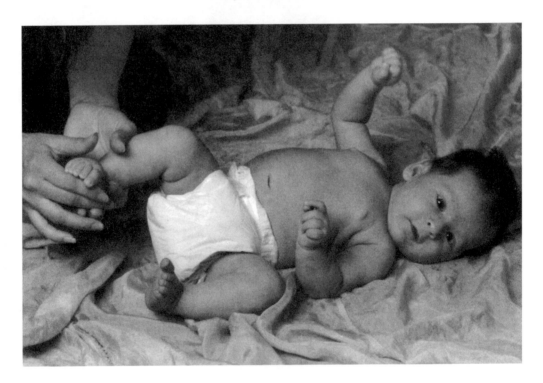

Fabric Feel

Rub your baby's arms and legs with different textures, like silk, velvet, satin, wool, flannel, and terry cloth. Describe each one as you gently touch your baby.

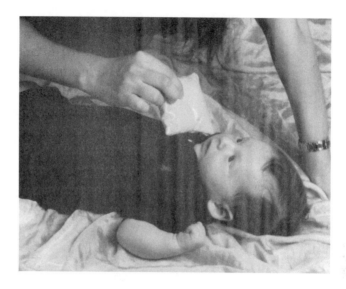

Light Touch

Stroke your baby gently with a paintbrush, a feather, or a cotton ball. Stroke different parts of his body, feet, hands, stomach, cheeks, and forehead. He will respond with a contented expression, or even a smile.

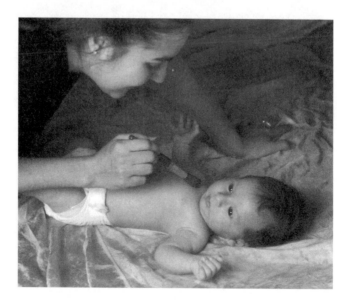

Exercising

Up and Down, In and Out

With your baby lying on his back, lift his arms gently up and down over his head, and then in and out. Sing a song at the same time:

> *Up-up-up little one*
> *Stretching, stretching is such fun*
> *In and out, let us go.*
> *Not too fast and not too slow.*

Bicycle Fun

Lie your baby on his back and gently move his legs in a bicycle movement. Try singing a song like "The Wheels On The Bus Go Round and Round" as you exercise together.

Up Lift

Put your baby on his tummy on the floor. Get down on the floor with him and show him a bright toy as you call his name. This encourages your baby to lift his head and exercise his neck, back, and arm muscles.

Looking Up at Mommy

Try the same activity again but this time you lie on your back and put your baby on your tummy. Call to your baby and encourage him to lift his head to see you.

DAILY ROUTINES

Mealtime

Position Changes

Breast fed babies naturally change positions while nursing. If your baby is bottle fed, alternate sides so he can see things from a different perspective.

Covered Bottle

If your baby is not breast feeding, slip a cover over his bottle and let him feel the bottle as he sucks. Bottle covers can be bought in stores, but a tennis sock works just as well.

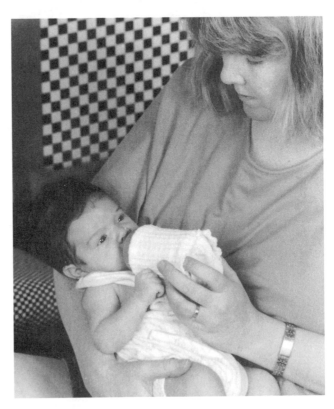

Bright Towel

Place a brightly colored towel over your shoulder while feeding the baby, or wear a bright scarf. Your baby will enjoy looking sometimes at your face, and sometimes at the towel. If your baby is distracted by the towel, you may not want to use it until feeding is over.

Bathtime

Loving Touch

After a bath, give your baby a massage. Select a favorite lullaby to sing during the massage. Your singing and your touching will combine to make your baby feel relaxed and secure.

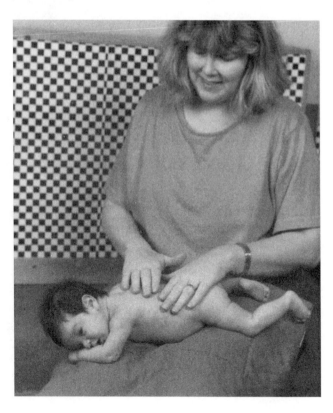

Diaper Time

Diversion

Hang some lightweight toys over the baby's changing table. He will stay still for a moment as he rediscovers each toy.

Blowing

Blow warm breath on arms and tummy. As your baby focuses attention on different parts of his body, he learns more about himself.

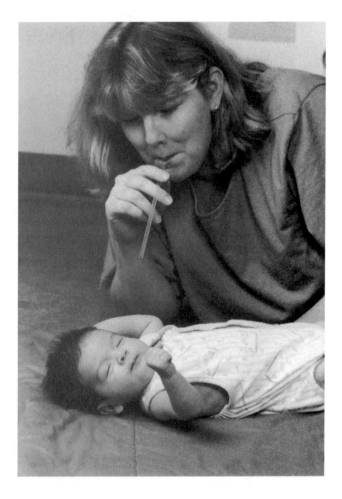

Quiet Time

Fluttering Ribbons

Attach short lengths of colored ribbons to a plastic ring. Hang the ring over your baby's crib, near an open window or an air-conditioning vent that will set the ring in motion. Your baby will enjoy watching the movement as he falls asleep.

Rest Awhile

Let your baby rest on your chest. Your rhythmic breathing and voice vibrations are soothing and comforting for your baby. You'll both enjoy the closeness.

TWO MONTHS

Baby's Viewpoint

Your two-month-old baby has made the adjustment to life outside the womb and is ready to face new challenges. Her periods of alertness last longer now and she is ready and eager to take in new information.

Most likely, your two-month-old awakens hungry and lets you know with a piercing cry. Comfortable and satisfied after her feeding, she is ready to play.

The face-to-face conversations described in the one month section continue, but with a subtle change. Although you are still the one who initiates and maintains the exchange, your baby has learned how to signal a pause. She alternates between looking at you and turning away, and, in this way, she is able to keep "conversing" for a longer time without getting overloaded.

Another important change at two months old is the frequency of smiling. At three weeks, a baby is most likely to smile at the sound of a familiar voice. At four weeks, a baby is most likely to smile at a familiar face. Now, at two months, both new and familiar faces elicit your baby's smile.

MOTOR SKILLS

Although no major motor milestones are achieved between one month and two months, there is a significant qualitative change in the way your baby moves her body. Whether she is at rest or at play, random, uncoordinated movements are few and far between, and the movements that we do see appear to be in your baby's control. Put to the breast for nursing, your baby no longer depends on reflex behavior to guide her to the nipple. After a few adjustments of head and neck she grasps the nipple with her lips and immediately starts to suck.

Your baby's improved sucking ability is not only apparent during nursing. In between feedings, a two-month-old baby will suck at almost anything that is placed in her mouth: her own hand, a pacifier, the corner of a blanket, or mother's finger. She knows the difference, however, between sucking for exercise and sucking to satisfy hunger. When she is not hungry, she will suck contentedly on the pacifier. When she is ready for nursing, she spits out the pacifier and cries.

Another sucking achievement of many two-month-old babies is purposeful and coordinated thumb sucking. At a younger age your baby sucked her thumb if it happened to land in her mouth. When the thumb fell out, she cried. Now, at two months old, your baby succeeds in getting both the hand and mouth under her control.

Because your baby still has a strong grasp reflex, it is easy to place a rattle into her hand. She may show interest in the rattle by shaking the hand that is doing the holding. You may even see your baby bring the rattle to her mouth. She probably views the rattle as an extension of her hand, however, and not as an object to be sucked, for when the rattle drops from her hand, she shows no sign of being upset.

In addition to improved sucking skill, your two-month-old shows a definite improvement in head control. By now, most babies will lift their heads up when lying on their stomach and can hold their head upright for a few seconds when they are held in a standing position. An especially strong baby may be able to support herself on her arms when she is lying on her stomach.

Arms and legs are more active now. Your baby extends her arms above her head in play. She twists her head and body from side to side. She moves her arms and legs up and down in a kind of rhythmic motion. Some babies, when lying on their stomachs, will begin to make crawling movements with their knees, using first one knee and then the other.

SEEING, HEARING, AND FEELING

A clear example of the ability to modify behavior in response to new information is the achievement of eye-hand coordination. At first, your baby examines her hand much as she would a new mobile—looking it up and down, inspecting the finger, the thumb, the sleeve of her nightgown. Gradually she discovers that she can increase the fun of hand-watching by moving her hand around. By the end of the second month, she may open and close her fingers, focusing her whole attention on watching a hand in action. It seems that she is aware that the hand she is looking at belongs to her, and that she can make it perform.

A two-month-old also is able to follow an object visually when it is several feet away. She is particularly adept at this if the object she is watching is swinging or fluttering, or if it happens to be an older sister or brother. By the end of the second month, most babies have established a clear connection between seeing and hearing in a familiar situation. They may associate a pleasant sound with a bell. When they hear the tinkling, they turn to look for its source.

Hearing, like vision, becomes more sophisticated in the third month. A baby becomes attentive to sounds, even soft ones—the telephone ring, the window shade flopping, the sound of Mommy's footsteps. As she did at an earlier age, your baby tends to freeze when first hearing an interesting sound. Her legs stop kicking, and her arms stop waving. Then, as your baby finds the source of the sound, she resumes the active movement of arms and legs.

Finally, with her hands open most of the time, your baby has new opportunities to find out how things feel. She seems already to notice the difference between hard and soft, and enjoys the feeling of something soft placed in her hand. As your baby continues to explore these tactile sensations, she stores up new information about the outside world.

KNOWING YOUR BABY

By the third month, your baby has mastered the art of smiling and will smile at anyone who bends over the crib. In fact, she smiles at anything that looks like a face. A Pinocchio puppet, a witch's mask, and a plate with two eyes will be greeted with the same smiling response. At about the same time your baby learns to smile, she begins to make talking sounds. This developmental stage is the beginning of babbling. Your baby will start by saying "ah-ah-ee-ee" or "eh-eh" as a sort of experiment, and then repeat the string of sounds over and over again. She seems to be intrigued with the sounds she is producing, and will often stay contentedly in her crib listening to her own voice.

When an adult joins the vocal play, the baby is delighted. The adult imitates the baby's sounds, the baby coos back, and a kind of "conversation" begins. In addition, parents appear to enjoy mirroring the facial expressions of their two-month-olds. If the baby opens up her mouth, her mother opens up her own mouth. If the baby squints her eyes, the mother squints her eyes. This behavior provides the baby with feed-back that helps her learn about herself.

Your baby now needs adults for more than food and comfort. A propped-up bottle is no substitute for a talking, laughing, singing, touch-ing parent. Your baby needs people to play with her and to respond to what she does. When you talk with, smile with, and coo back to your baby during each of her waking periods, you are help-ing her develop important social skills.

Suggested Activities

SETTING THE STAGE

Dress Down

When you begin an activity period with your baby, make sure that her clothing is loose—the less she wears, the better. Remember that a baby is more active when she is a little cool.

Baby Bounce

Make sure that your baby has something interesting to look at during her waking hours. Change her perspective by sitting her in an infant seat or in a baby bounce chair, or by holding her in an infant carrier.

Conversation

Imitate the sounds your baby makes. Listen for her to repeat the sound, then imitate it again. Make sure to look in the baby's eyes during these conversations.

Sing Along

Learn some little jingles to go along with different activities such as bathing, feeding, and exercising. To "Twinkle Twinkle Little Star":

Splash splash splash, my little fish
Make a big splash if you wish.
Splash the water all around
Listen to the splashing sound.

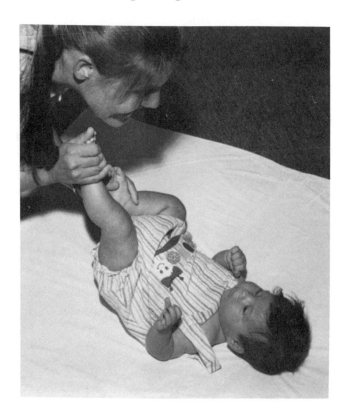

Sibling Fun

Give your baby time to be with his older sisters and brothers. Their attention will entertain and stimulate her.

Camera Ready!

Remember to keep a loaded camera handy. A photo album is your best way to record the day-by-day changes and recapture the happy moments.

Visiting

Your baby will enjoy accompanying you as you make visits to stores and friends. The new sights, sounds, and smells serve to stimulate your baby.

SEEING, LISTENING, AND FEELING

Hand Watch

Make your baby a pair of wrist bands or buy a pair of brightly colored infant socks. Sometimes put the band or sock on the right hand, sometimes on the left, and sometimes on both. As your baby moves her hands around in front of her eyes, she will discover how to manage her hands so that they stay where her eyes can watch them. You can also sew a bell securely to the sock so your baby can make a connection between her actions, the sound, and the movement of the sock.

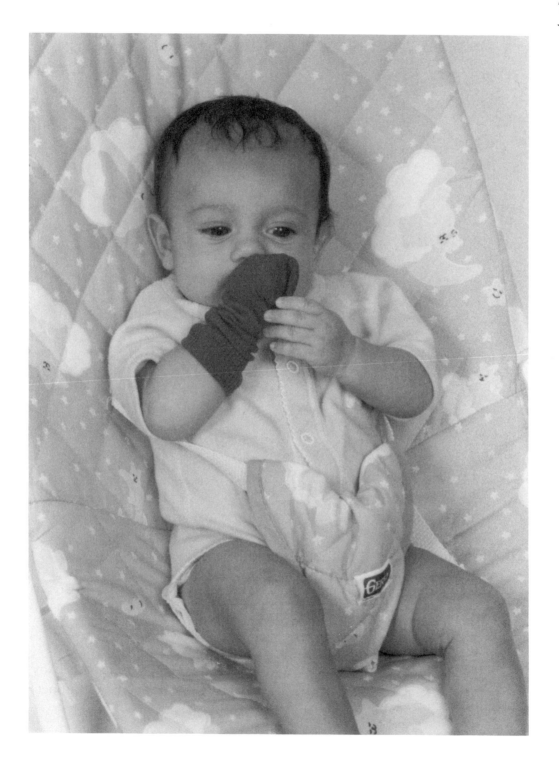

Hand Puppet

Move the hand puppet up and down, back and forth, and around in a circle within the baby's line of vision. Giving your baby practice in tracking develops her visual skills.

Squeak Toy

Put a squeak toy in your baby's hand. The accidental squeak will help her become aware of what her hand is doing.

Finger Puppet

Put a puppet on your finger and let the baby watch it dance. The sillier looking the puppet, the more your baby seems to enjoy it.

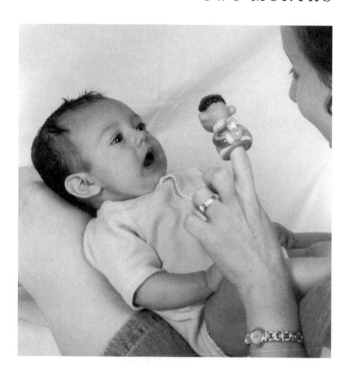

Plate Puppet

Make a reversible puppet out of a paper plate and a stick. Put a happy face on one side and a sad face on the other side. Move the plate puppet back and forth in front of your baby. Show her the sad side and then the happy side. You will

find that your baby loves to look at a face, and she will soon begin to talk to it. The fact that the face keeps changing keeps up her interest.

Cradle Gym

String a cradle gym over her crib or cradle. Change the objects that are attached to the gym. Remember that your baby enjoys bright colors, interesting shapes, and things that move easily.

Changing Patterns

Paste contact paper or wrapping paper with different colors and patterns on all sides of a small diaper box. Loop a ribbon through the corner of the box and suspend it over your baby's crib. After a while your baby will reach up and bat at the box.

Upside-Down Daddy

Lay your baby on her back in Mother's lap. Let Daddy sit in a chair at right angles to Mother. This gives the baby an interesting upside down view of Daddy's face.

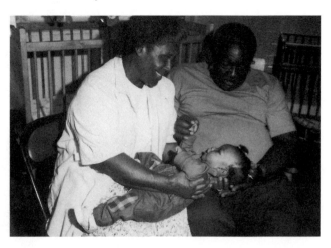

New Look

Change the pictures on the wall by the crib or feeding chair. A bulletin board is ideal.

Rattle Shake

Your baby is getting more efficient at tracking with her eyes and attending to different sounds. Let her practice these skills by moving a rattle at different speeds and in different directions as you sing this song:

> *Shake it high and shake it low.*
> *Shake it fast and shake it slow.*
> *Shake that rattle, follow that sound.*
> *Shake that rattle, see what you found.*
>   (Give baby the rattle).

Up and Down

Sing songs to your baby that have up and down actions in them. As you move your baby up, down and around, she will see her world from different perspectives.

> *Here we go up, up, up* (lift baby up).
> *Here we go down, down, down*
>   (put baby down).
> *Here we go front and back*
>   (turn baby around).
> *Here we go round and round*
>   (hold baby and spin around).

Greeting

Call out to baby before you enter the room. Your baby will learn to recognize your voice and anticipate your arrival.

Rattle Hold

Place a rattle in your baby's hand. She will learn to recognize that the rattle is there. Sometimes she will shake it and sometimes she will bring it up to her mouth before she lets it drop. Be sure you give both hands a turn.

Feeling Sticks

Because your baby's hands are open a great deal of the time, she will enjoy experimenting with different textures. Glue some textured fabric on old-fashioned wooden clothespins. Bits of burlap, satin, velvet, and corduroy work well. Talk about each texture as you hand them to your baby. Is it soft? Is it bumpy? These clothespins are ideal for encouraging grasping skills.

Exercising

Pompom Toss

With your baby lying on her back in front of you, hold up large colored pompoms. Let them drop

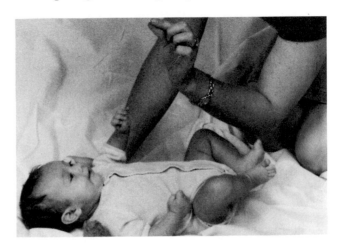

to her tummy and announce, "Here comes another pompom!" As your baby matures, she will
begin to anticipate the pompom falling.

Bicycle Play

Exercising your baby's legs is important. Lay
her on her back, hold her feet in the palms of
your hands, and push them gently in a circular
fashion. Soon she will be pushing your hands!
Adding a song increases the fun:

> *Bicycle, Bicycle Baby* (use your baby's name)
> *Bicycle, Bicycle girl*
> *BOOP, BOOP* (lift your baby's bottom up
>   by holding her feet)

Kicking Arena

The bottom end of the crib provides an excellent
rod for hanging an assortment of kicking objects.
Hang things at different lengths and try objects
with different textures. A large pompom and a
bell provide your baby with a soft, quiet object
and a hard, noisy object. Put her on her back
near the end of the crib so her feet can reach the
kicking arena. Let her experiment.

DAILY ROUTINES

Mealtime

Rocking Chair

If you haven't yet found how wonderful your rocking chair can be at feeding time, try it now. Holding your baby close, feeding, and rocking are relaxing for both you and your baby.

Daddy's Turn

Make sure that Dad has some time to feed baby. If you are breast feeding, let Dad offer a water bottle if your baby drinks one. If you express your milk and need to go out during your baby's mealtime, Dad has the perfect opportunity!

Bathtime

Splashtime

Let your baby splash her hands and feet in her warm bath water. Pat dry with towel after bath. Your baby learns about her world through her sense of touch.

Bathing Beauty

After your baby's bath, sit on the floor in front of a full-length mirror and let her see herself in the mirror. If she discovers her image in the mirror, tickle her or swing her gently. She will probably be attentive to this smiling figure. Watching a smiling baby in the mirror will help to sustain her interest.

Massage Time

"Squeeze gently, twist gently" is a relaxing massage technique. With a small amount of vegetable oil in your hands, hold your baby's leg up as if you were holding a baseball bat, and gently massage her legs. Massage her arms in the same way.

Diaper Time

Feeling Mural

Hang a textured mural next to the changing table. A collage of materials will do just fine (towel, silky scarf, fuzzy wool, shiny aluminum foil). As you change your baby, talk to her about them.

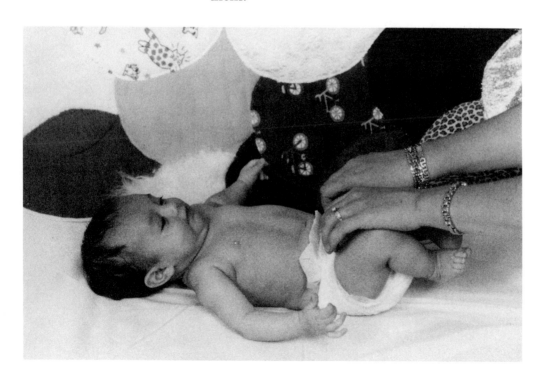

Mirror Play

Try changing your baby in front of a mirror. Stick mirrored wall tiles next to the changing table. Your baby is fascinated by her image. As she matures she will grow to enjoy this mirror play even more.

Feather Duster Fun

Keep a new feather duster near the changing table. While your baby is undressed, tickle her body parts as you name them.

> *Tickle, tickle, tickle*
> *Baby's nose today.*
> *Tickle, tickle, tickle*
> *We love tickle play.*

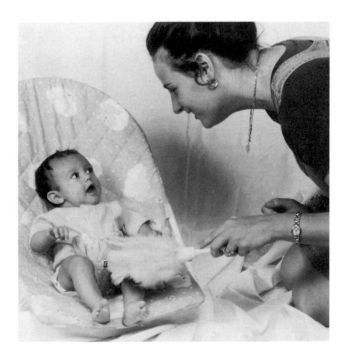

Punch Ball

Your baby spends a good deal of time on the changing table—probably looking at the white ceiling. Create an interesting, appealing environment for her by hanging an inflatable ball from the ceiling. At first your baby will watch it as it sways; soon she will make attempts to bat at it.

Quiet Time

Beach Ball

Inflate a beach ball almost to its fullest capacity. Gently place baby face down on the beach ball, with tummy resting on the ball. Place your hands on her hips and slowly rock the baby back and forth. Many babies find this a relaxing activity that gets them ready for sleep.

TV Time

If your family enjoys watching TV, your baby will enjoy sitting with you for a short period of time. She will enjoy the sound and movement, as well as the chance to be with the family.

Audiotaping

If you happen to have a tape recorder, it's fun to use with the baby. Tape record the sounds your baby makes. Play back the tape to the baby often. Your baby may fall asleep as she talks along with the tape.

CHAPTER 4

THREE MONTHS

Baby's Viewpoint

The fourth month is exciting for your baby and you. As your infant spends more time awake each day, he has more time to explore his surroundings. His eyes catch sight of the mobile hanging over his crib. He looks from right to left, then left to right, and usually examines each piece. If you move a rattle across the crib, he follows it intently with his eyes. When it disappears from sight, baby continues to stare at the place where it was. Is baby registering surprise because it disappeared, or does he believe that looking will bring the rattle back?

Your baby's favorite toy at this time is himself. He seems to be constantly trying to learn about himself. His fingers explore his own eyes, nose, mouth, and chin. He rubs his hand along his cheeks, patting, pinching, and sometimes scratching. Many babies at this age will join their hands together and let each hand take a turn playing with the other.

In many ways the fourth month is a time of transition. At one and two months, your baby's primary energy is spent in self-regulation. His interaction with the world outside himself is focused on taking in information. He absorbs the world with eyes, ears, hands, and mouth and is fascinated by his many discoveries. Now he is ready to explore his world in a more active way. He is getting ready to be an impetus for action—a prime mover in a responsive environment. We see this first "action oriented" behavior in the baby's social interaction. He no longer waits to be spoken to and smiled at. He initiates responses. He seeks out faces, then smiles and babbles, and makes the world smile back.

MOTOR SKILLS

Important new motor skills emerge during the fourth month. Your baby is learning to reach out and grasp an object. He is also learning how to shift his weight when he is on his tummy, setting one arm free to reach out. Although your baby may miss the mark when he tries to grasp a toy, with opportunity and practice he is certain to master this skill.

Even before your baby is successful in grasping a toy, he will bat at a cradle gym that is strung across his crib. This batting activity follows a regular pattern. Your baby bats at the gym, stops, observes, and then resumes his batting with increasing vigor.

Piaget, a Swiss psychologist who has studied infant behavior, suggests that the first time the baby bats at the gym it is accidental. But when he hits it, the gym moves up and down in an interesting way. The baby bats some more in order to make this interesting event happen again. In this effort to make something interesting happen again, we see the baby's growing capacity for purposeful behavior.

Differences in rates of development, particularly in the motor area, can be very evident during the fourth month. While an active baby may already be turning from stomach to back, other babies are still limited to energetic bicycle movements with legs and arms. All babies, no matter how old or how active, must be carefully watched. No baby should be left alone on a changing table, and all babies must be securely strapped into their infant seat or bouncing chair.

SEEING, HEARING, AND FEELING

During the fourth month, your baby shows an increased interest in his own hands and anything that they happen to be holding. He holds an object in view for a longer time now and inspects it with his eyes. Often he lies quietly on his back staring intensely, first at one hand, then the other. If you place a rattle in his hand, he will first look at it and then bring it up to his mouth. If you hold an object directly in front of him, he may reach for it and grasp it with two hands.

Your baby is beginning, at the same time, to anticipate future events. Just a few weeks ago he continued to cry with hunger until the nipple was in his mouth. Now he reacts as soon as he sees the bottle. His crying may stop or may get louder. Your baby is clearly attaching a meaning to a visual stimulus. The bottle he is looking at is not just a passing image. It is something that belongs in his mouth.

Along with this new awareness of the function of objects, there is a new reaction to objects that drop out of sight. Your baby will follow a rattle that is taken away and then stare at the spot where it was last seen. He is remembering the rattle, but he doesn't yet know that looking won't bring it back.

The three-month-old's impressive ability to hold onto a memory is demonstrated by his smiling behavior. In an experimental situation, babies as young as six weeks old will smile more for an animated, talking mother than any other animated talking adult. The three-month-old continues to smile more for his parent than to a different adult, but at a new level of sophistication. Now the baby smiles immediately at the appearance of his mother's face, even when mother is silent. His smile is more than a pleasant association, it is a smile of recognition.

Association between sight and sound is now mastered. Baby turns his head toward the sound of his mother's voice. A jingling rattle attracts his attention, and he will turn his head completely around in order to keep it in sight. He particularly enjoys musical toys, radio, tapes, and even the beat of a metronome. He will turn toward the object that makes the noise even when it isn't moving.

With his hand open most of the time now, your baby uses his fingers for active exploration. The soft border of the blanket slips between his fingers, and he rubs his thumb up and down to continue the pleasant sensation. Your baby is no longer passively enjoying a variety of sensations. He provides his own pleasure by actively selecting the sensations he enjoys.

KNOWING YOUR BABY

Your three-month-old baby has become a social being. His response to attention, his delight with imitative play, his active vocalizations, and his out-loud chuckles are all signs of a need and readiness for social interaction. It is during this period that parents and babies spend long periods of time talking back and forth to each other. You talk and smile, and your baby babbles and smiles back. An outsider watching this intense conversation will have difficulty deciding who, in fact, is the leader.

These intimate conversations result in a closer than ever bond between you and your baby. Parents not only identify their baby's different cries, they interpret a whole range of sounds that their baby makes: a whimper of hunger, a laugh of delight, a gurgling of vocal play. Babies, in turn, identify parents by sight as well as feel. Although your baby will be quick to return other smiles, his most radiant smile will be reserved for you.

An exciting development between three and four months is a rapid increase in vocalization. Your baby will spend a lot of time practicing his newly found vocal talents. Now his vowel and consonant sounds are quite distinguishable, and his repertoire may include sounds of "1," "n," "m," "b," and "p." He produces his consonant sounds most often when he is content and relaxed.

Babble conversations, although certainly an important developmental event, are not the only

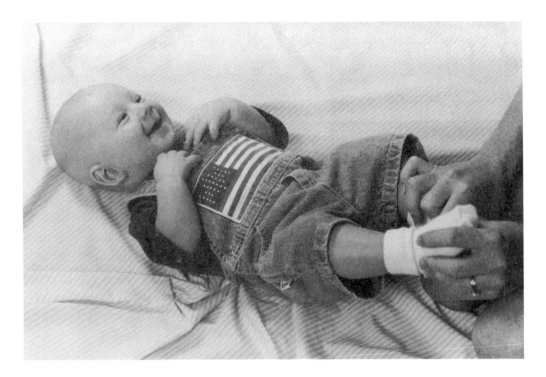

way you communicate with your baby. You and your baby constantly send messages back and forth to each other through facial expressions, body language, and actions. One of the messages your baby may be communicating to you is, "Don't put me down, even if I am asleep, I need you." When your baby was younger, we suggested that you respond to him without concern about "spoiling." You should still not be concerned about spoiling your baby, but it is important to help babies learn to acquire internal resources. In other words, just as your baby is sending out the message, "Don't put me down, I need you," you need to send a message back, "I am putting you down, I love you, and you're fine."

In an earlier chapter we talked about the importance of helping your baby accept a pacifier. Babies who enjoy a pacifier at three months have a ready-made self-comforting strategy that helps them settle down in a crib. Another way to help your baby accept the transition from your arms to the crib is to put him down in the crib when he is feeling awake, relaxed, and happy. As you place him in the crib, continue talking and smiling, keep your face close to his, and maintain eye contact. If you remain calm, cheerful, and in control when you place your baby in a crib or infant seat, he will learn from you that he, too, is in control.

Suggested Activities

SETTING THE STAGE

Cradle Gym

Your baby is eager to practice his new batting skill. Hang a toy with balls, rings, and spinners across your baby's crib. Position your baby so that he can activate this cradle gym with his arms and then with his feet. A cradle gym that has a disk with a face attached to it makes batting even more fun.

Conversations

Carry on conversations with your baby at every opportunity. Use different tones of voice, high, low, loud, soft, laughing, soothing. When your baby "talks" to you, wait until his "sentence" is over and then imitate his sounds. The more you talk with your baby, the more babbling he will do. Use your baby's name frequently. When singing or reciting nursery rhymes, substitute your baby's name for the word "baby."

Outside Play

Being outside is a wonderful change of scenery for you and your baby. Place your baby under a tree. He will enjoy listening to the rustle of leaves and watching the play of light and shadow as the leaves move with the wind. Birds give your baby practice in tracking, and airplanes make novel and interesting noises.

Song Time

During the first year, it is important to sing to your baby. As your baby grows older, you will find yourself changing the ways you sing. With the newborn you sang softly, steadily, and held your baby close. With a three-month-old, chang-

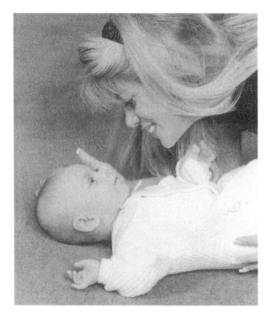 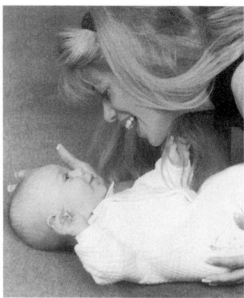

ing your volume, pace, and rhythm, and letting your baby watch your face, makes singing very special.

Making Discoveries

Pet Watching

Let your baby have the opportunity to see your pet as it moves around. Dogs, cats, and birds are especially exciting to watch. The slow movement of fish in a tank are soothing and relaxing.

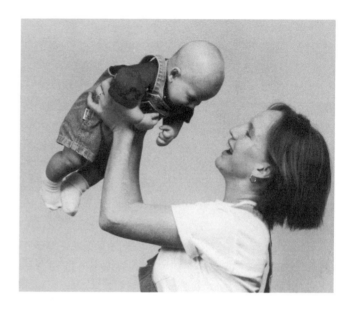

New Perspectives

Lift your baby up and down in your arms so that he can watch your face from different perspectives. Observe his reactions. How does he react when you appear upside down or with a silly expression?

String Toys

String toys within your baby's reach so he can practice batting. Although a playpen is useful for this purpose, its usefulness is short-lived. You can accomplish the same goals by stringing the toy from chair to chair, on a stroller, or on a car seat. Remember to keep the strings short to be safe around your baby.

Rhythms

Your baby enjoys music and rhythm. Play a tape with strong rhythm. Tap out the beat of the song using a tambourine, two clothespins, or your

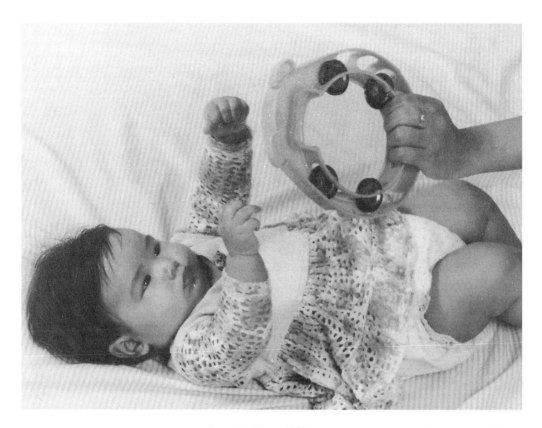

hands. Try different songs, some fast, some slow, some loud, some soft. After a while, your baby will recognize a marked change in the rhythm.

Shake-Shake

Place a wrist band on your baby's wrist with a bell sewn securely inside. Shake his hand gently until he looks at it. Change the wrist band to the other hand and repeat with more shaking. You can also put the wrist band on your baby's ankles. These activities increase body awareness and improve eye-hand coordination.

Buzzing Bees

Try singing this chant with your baby to encourage more babbling. Remember to maintain eye contact as you sing!

> *Ba Ba Ba Bumble Bee*
> *First you say Ba to me*
> *Then I say Ba to you*
> *Ba Ba Ba Bumble Bee.*

Give your baby a chance to respond with his own "b" sound!

Texture Glove

Make yourself a pair of texture gloves. Use an old glove and tape a different fabric around each finger. Use fabrics with varied textures, such as velcro, satin, silk, feathers, and terry cloth. Let your baby grasp each of the fingers.

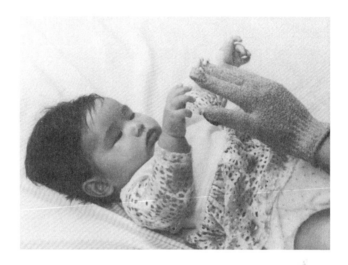

Surprise Songs

Learn a variety of songs with surprise endings to sing to your baby. Through repetition, your baby will begin to anticipate the surprise. Try this one while baby is sitting on your lap:

> (Bounce baby up and down on
>   your knees.)
> *Trot trot to Boston*
> *Trot trot to Lynn*
> (Open up your legs and catch your baby
>   as he drops through.)
> *You'd better watch out or*
> *You might fall IN!*

MOTOR SKILLS

Leg Play

Lift up the baby's legs and then let them fall as you recite:

> *Hippety Hippety Hippety-Hop*
> *Hippety Hippety and then we flop.*

Sit-Up Game

Pull the baby up gently and slowly by his arms in a seesaw game. Here's a chant to use with the game:

> *Up my little Kenneth comes*
> *Down my Kenneth goes,*
> *Peek around, have you found*
> *Kenneth's wiggly toes.*

The game strengthens your baby's stomach muscles and at the same time lets him see the world from different points of view.

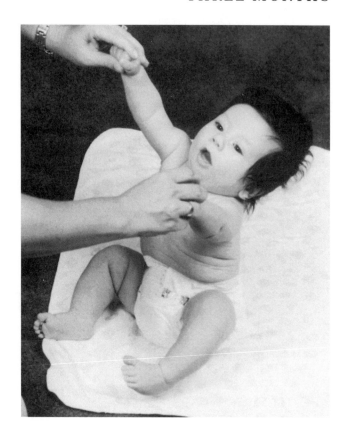

Row Row Row Your Baby

Using the familiar verse, "Row, row, row, your boat," cradle your baby in your lap facing you. Support his back and head with your arms. Gently rock baby back and forth while singing.

> *Row row row your baby*
> *Gently down the stream*
> *Merrily, merrily, merrily, merrily*
> *Life is but a dream.*

Make sure to sing slowly so that the actions can match the words.

Foot Push

Place your baby on his stomach on the floor. Kneeling behind him, place the palms of your hands against the soles of his feet. Your baby will ease himself forward by pushing first against one of your hands and then the other. This pushing exercise will help get your baby ready to crawl on his own.

Turning Over

Between three and four months, most babies are beginning to turn over. Usually babies begin by rolling from front to back. Next, babies will master back to side and finally from back to front. Help your baby practice these emerging skills. Put your hands under his shoulders, and gently rock him back and forth. When he is on his side, hesitate and let him try to turn himself the rest of the way over.

Roly-poly
My little Erik,

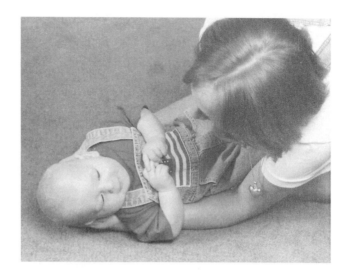

Roly-poly
We'll have fun!
Roly-poly
My little baby,
You have to roll before you RUN!

As you sing, roll your baby back and forth to the rhythm of the music—any tune will do. At this age, some babies wake themselves up at night because they flip over and can't flip back. Helping your baby learn to roll over may solve this problem.

Solving Problems

Rattle Play

Continue placing a slim-handled rattle in your baby's hands. Shake your baby's hand gently. See if he will lift his arm to see what is making the noise.

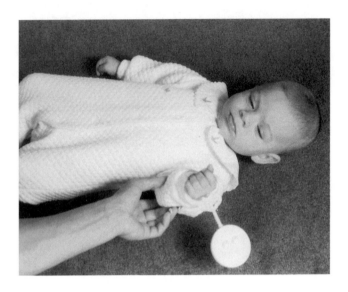

Tracking Fun

Lay your baby on his tummy on the floor. Roll a bright, attractive ball from side to side about two feet in front of your baby. With a little practice your baby will be able to coordinate eye and hand movements and reach toward the ball.

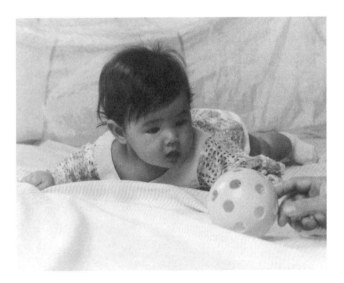

Bell Search

Ring a bell that makes a pleasant tinkling sound while baby is watching. Sound the bell again on the side just out of baby's line of vision. See if your baby will search for the bell with his eyes. Try this game with a rattle and a squeak toy.

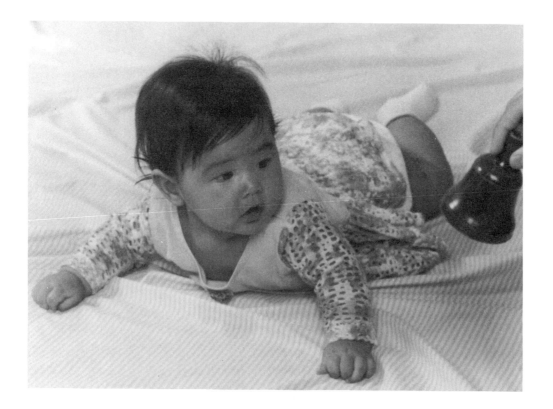

Beach Ball Batting

Inflate a beach ball or a punching ball and tie a string to the nozzle. Lay your baby on his back and hold the beach ball above his legs. Can your baby kick the ball with his feet? Now, hold it above his hands. Will he reach for it?

Merry-Go-Round

Put a bright ring on a string and circle it slowly in one direction around your baby's head until it's out of sight. After a while, your baby will anticipate the ring's reappearance and search for it with his eyes.

DAILY ROUTINES

Mealtime

Touching Time

Your baby needs to be held and cuddled as he eats. There's no place for bottle propping! Make sure your baby's arms and hands are free to touch and explore as he is feeding. Encourage him to touch your face by gently rubbing your eyes, nose, mouth, and hair with his hands. Draping a soft, silky scarf around your neck will also encourage visual and tactile stimulation.

Bathtime

Make bathtime part of your baby's routine. A typical schedule might be bath, massage, dress, feed, and sing to baby before you put him to sleep. Find the routine that works best for you and your baby. You will both appreciate the routine, and baby will find it easier to go to sleep when he knows what to expect.

Singing in the Bath

Use bathtime to further develop your baby's self-concept. Sing songs about his body parts as you wash them. Try this one for fun (to the tune of "London Bridge is Falling Down").

Head and shoulders, knees and toes,
knees and toes
knees and toes,
Head and shoulders, knees and toes,
Eyes and ears and chin and mouth and nose!

Ball Play

Put some brightly colored balls in the baby's bath. As he reaches for them he will have fun watching them bob up and down.

Bath Togetherness

For a relaxing change of pace, take a warm bath with your baby. Holding him on his back and rock him back and forth. Make sure you have someone to help you out of the tub. Wet babies are slippery!

Diaper Time

Naked Baby

Give baby opportunities to be without his diaper at times. Put him on a washable surface in case of an accident. Being naked allows your baby to become more aware of himself. It's also a perfect time for some gentle massaging.

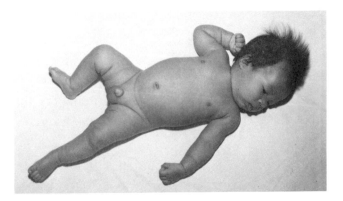

After Bath Exercise

Use diaper time for more exercising with baby. Try singing this song as you move his body parts:

If you're happy and you know it, kick your feet.
If you're happy and you know it kick your feet.
If you're happy and you know it and you really
want to show it,
If you're happy and you know it kick your feet.

Also, sing "if you're happy and you know it . . . clap your hands, find your nose, tickle your tummy, or give a kiss."

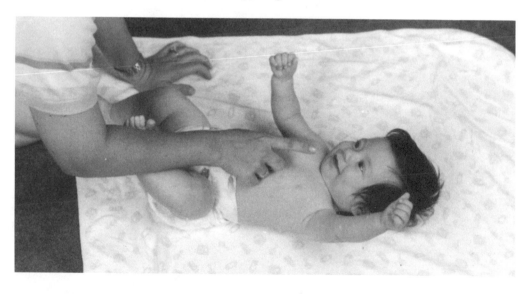

Animal Sounds

Whisper in your baby's ear. Make different animal sounds—moo, bark, meow, peep, etc. He will notice the different sounds, smile, and perhaps even laugh aloud.

Quiet Time

Bubble Watch

Blow bubbles for your baby with liquid bubbles and a wand. Your baby will love watching the bubbles as they slowly float by.

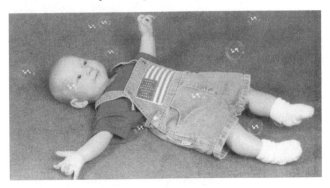

Phone Time

When you speak on the telephone, hold your baby close and look at him. Your baby will enjoy watching and listening to you. He'll even think your conversation is just for him!

Tick-Tock

Let a clock tick near your baby. The rhythmic ticking gives your baby an awareness of rhythm and may help to soothe him.

CHAPTER 5

FOUR MONTHS

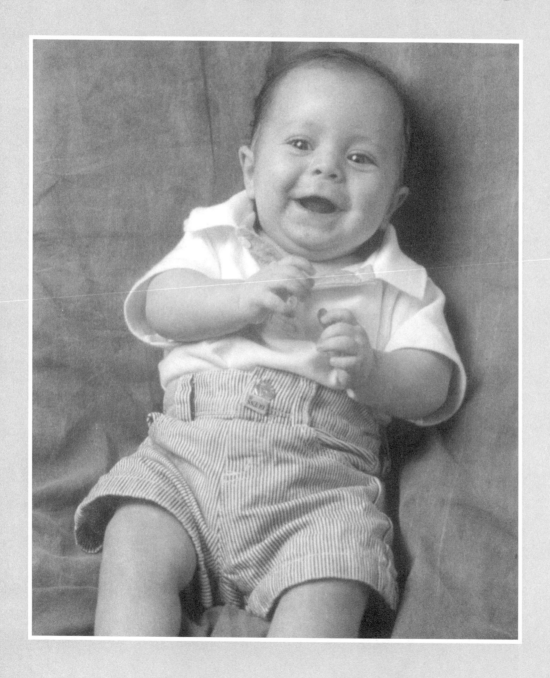

Baby's Viewpoint

The fifth month is an exciting time for babies and parents. Your baby has made the transition from passive observer to active explorer. She is reaching, grasping, and playing with toys. She is also reaching out to people, engaging in "conversations," and chuckling with delight in response to a playful parent.

Your baby will find new ways to play with toys strung across her crib. As you watch your baby playing with her crib toy, you will discover that she is involved in a kind of routine. She grasps and releases the ring of the gym, watches the mobile twirl, then attempts to grasp it again. This grasp, look, then grasp again routine is not, of course, limited to the cradle gym in the crib. Your baby is now ready to play with many toys. As she manipulates each new object within her reach, she is asking a wordless question: "What is this thing in my hand and what can I make it do?"

These new developments in your baby's interaction with objects are matched by the new developments we see in social interactions. Your four-month-old is learning to initiate a social exchange. Instead of waiting for a visitor to make the overtures, your baby coos, babbles, and smiles as soon as the visitor arrives. Because nothing is quite as captivating as a cooing, smiling baby, the visitor is compelled to respond.

MOTOR SKILLS

Many babies at four months old have learned to move around. Your baby may be squirming up to the top or down to the bottom of her crib. When you put her tummy down on a blanket, she may try to edge forward by pushing down with one foot and then the other, or pulling with her arms. When babies begin to scoot, they are likely to edge backwards or sideways before they manage to go forward.

Many babies can roll now from stomach to back. Some babies can also manage a back-to-stomach roll. Your baby now sits up quite successfully when propped on pillows, and may even take some tentative steps when held up and supported. Contrary to popular belief, standing a baby on her feet before she can successfully bear her weight does not produce a bow-legged baby.

Your baby's hands are now busy reaching and grasping. As long as she is able to see both her hand and the object at the same time, she is able to grasp at just about anything she sees. This grasp, however, is quite crude. The thumb and fingers are not yet independent agents. Your baby holds an object by pressing her fingers against the palm of her hand. She will scoop up, rather than pick up, an object lying on a table.

As your baby practices her newly acquired grasping skills, she will spend relatively long stretches of time actively engaged in playing with a toy. A cradle gym stretched across her crib, with a dangling ring and toys that rattle, is especially attractive to her. As she grasps the ring, lets go, and grasps it again, her efforts are rewarded by the jingling sounds.

SEEING, HEARING, AND FEELING

Your four-month-old's improved eye-hand coordination is, in part, a reflection of improved visual skills. The younger baby's visual system, like a fixed focus camera, could see objects clearly only if they were 8 to 12 inches away. Now your baby can change her focus so that she sees things sharply at different distances. Because of this newly acquired skill, she will be excited when visiting new places and seeing new sights.

An unbreakable mirror hanging from a cradle gym or attached to the side of her crib is a favorite toy at this age. Baby catches sight of her own image in the mirror, watches the movements of her hands and face, and smiles. She is not old enough to recognize that she is looking at herself, but she will have fun watching the smiling baby in the mirror.

Despite your baby's increased visual skill, her main means of exploring objects is with her mouth. She mouths an object as soon as she grasps it. Seeing, grasping, and mouthing seem to happen in rapid succession. After a while, she will add visual inspection to this routine. She will look at the object she has grasped before bringing it to her mouth.

Paralleling her new interest in visual exploration is a fascination with new sounds. The four-month-old has discovered that she can make different kinds of sounds come out of her mouth, and she enjoys listening to them. When she discovers a sound she particularly likes—a squeal, a raspberry, a cough—she practices it over and over again. Many four-month-olds also experiment with changes in volume, babbling very loudly or softly while listening to the effect they have created.

KNOWING YOUR BABY

At four months old, babies are delighted with visitors. They welcome a stranger with almost the same enthusiasm as they do a parent or sibling. As a matter of fact, they are delighted with faces in just about any form. Even the silliest looking mask or the oddest looking puppet are delightful playmates from the baby's point of view.

Although your four-month-old baby enjoys meeting new people, her way of interacting with new people is different from her way of interacting with you. Your baby not only responds more enthusiastically to your overtures, she is also more likely to explore your face. She explores with her fingers, touching your eyes, nose, mouth, and even a mustache. She pulls at a strand of hair. When you begin a conversation, she sticks her fingers in your mouth as if physically capturing your words.

At the same time your baby demonstrates this intense fascination with the words coming out of your mouth, her own repertoire of sounds is expanding. She masters most of the vowel sounds as well as a few of the consonants. At three months, babies of all languages and nationalities—even hearing impaired infants—sound alike. By four months we begin to see a change. Babies tune into the language they hear at home, and they practice making sounds from their home language.

Although a four-month-old baby may carry on a fine conversation with a bird mobile or a brightly colored rattle, she seems most enthusiastic when faced with a responsive audience. When you imitate your baby's babbling sounds, her babbling increases in volume and intensity, and you and your baby will enjoy a high-pitched conversation.

Parents, especially fathers, respond to the baby's enthusiastic verbalizations by providing physical stimulation. They hold the baby in the air, tickle her tummy, or give her a noisy kiss. Their baby is likely to respond to this intrusive stimulation with a burst of laughter. A surprise response from mom or dad, such as a cough or sneeze, will initiate a chuckle. Your baby will also begin to playfully cough to get your attention. She is truly using her emerging language skills to initiate your response.

Although the bursts of laughter of a four-month-old baby are fun to listen to, it is important to remember that, in babies, laughter and tears are very close together. The baby's laugh serves as a release valve for mounting tension. If the tension is too great, however, the laughter changes to crying. You are likely to see this quick switch from laughter to tears in a rough-house session with your baby. At one moment you lift your baby in the air and she laughs out loud. A second later, you lift her a little higher, and she bursts into tears. For the young baby, there is a fine line between enough and too much excitement. By reading the baby's cues, parents become adept at knowing just how much stimulation their baby can tolerate and enjoy.

Suggested Activities

INTRODUCTION

At four months old, your baby is reaching out. In a sense she is beginning to make decisions for herself. Does she want to reach for a rattle, solicit a smile, or practice her cooing sounds? Remember that the play ideas are only suggestions. Observe your baby as she plays with a rattle, or interacts with your spouse. What skills is she practicing? What new skills is she working on? What sorts of toys engage her attention? What makes her smile, and what makes her look stressed?

Your baby is your best guide. Select some of the play ideas we describe, or create your own activities in response to your baby's capabilities and preferences. You know your baby intimately, and you, better than anyone else, can describe what is best for you and your baby.

SETTING THE STAGE

Sitting Up

Babies enjoy seeing the world from different perspectives. Sitting up makes it easier for your baby to watch your movements and carry on a conversation. Find a way to let her sit in a propped position for at least a part of every day. Try a bouncy chair, a swing, or an infant seat. Your baby may be sturdy enough to switch positions in their infant carrier. Try a number of positions, such as facing outward, to see which she prefers.

Floor Time

Let your baby play on a firm, flat surface wearing only a diaper. Free from the restrictions of clothing and covers, she is able to perform her finest gymnastics.

Reaching Up

When your baby is in her infant seat, hang up interesting toys on strings to encourage her to reach. Equip her crib or playpen with an interesting cradle gym. It's particularly fun when the toys make noise.

When your baby is able to hold her own weight on her forearms and lift up her shoulders, try placing a baby mirror in front of her. She will have fun looking at her own reflection.

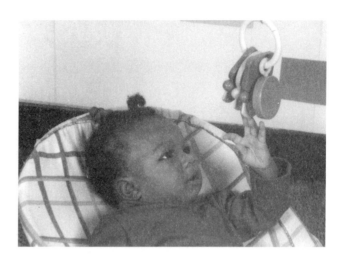

Grasping

Your baby is refining her grasping skills at the same time she is practicing reaching. Have a supply of different size rattles available to help her practice. Let her reach for the rattle, first with one hand, then with the other. Try holding the rattle lower and higher, closer and farther away. As your baby practices her grasping, she gets better and better at coordinating her hands and eyes.

Door Swing

This is the perfect age to use a swing that hangs from a door frame. Your baby is strong enough to sit comfortably but not strong enough to try to get out. She will enjoy swinging back and forth and waving her arms while you tickle her feet and carry on a conversation.

Now that your baby is spending more time awake, make sure that she has time to play with toys as well as people. Both kinds of experiences are important.

MAKING DISCOVERIES

Bubble Tracking

Your baby still enjoys watching bubbles float through the air. Blow bubbles when she is outside in her stroller. She will squeal with delight as she watches the bubbles float and pop.

Peek-a-Boo

Play peek-a-boo with your baby. Try placing your hands over your eyes, then over your baby's eyes. Place a blanket over your head and come out with "boo." Your baby will enjoy all variations of the game.

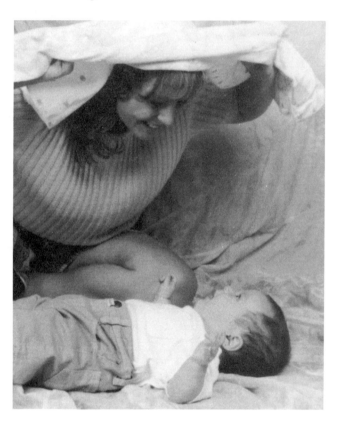

Back Talk

Tape record your baby's babbling and play it back to her. Tape record Mommy's and Daddy's voice and play this back, as well. See how your baby reacts when your voice comes from the tape recorder instead of from your mouth.

Car Crash

Build a cardboard hill for your baby. Let her watch a wheel toy slide down the hill. After a while, your baby will anticipate the crash as the toy slides down the hill.

Fabric Ball

Make a fabric ball by cutting several pieces of fabric into three-inch strips. Tie the strips of fabric together and secure them in the center with an extra strip. Your baby will enjoy holding the ball and feeling the different textures. Fabric balls with noise makers inside are also fun and are sold in most stores that carry baby toys.

Sock Play

Your baby is now interested in discovering the parts of her own body. Put a brightly colored sock on your baby's feet. At first your baby will just look at her feet, but after a while she will succeed in catching her foot—a very important conquest in her young life.

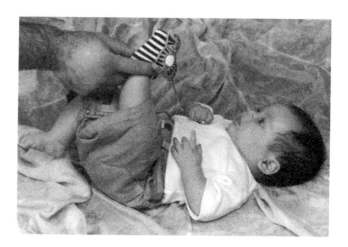

MOTOR SKILLS

Exercise Time

This is a good time for you and your baby to exercise together. Hold your baby at the waist, raise her in the air, jostle her up and down, then hold her upright in a standing position. Dance together to all types of music. It's fun and relaxing for both of you.

New Perspectives

Place a small pillow under your baby's tummy while she is on a rug. This will strengthen her neck and arm muscles.

Frog Kick

This exercise helps strengthen your baby's leg muscles and encourages crawling and creeping. While your baby is on her tummy:

1. Bend her knees up at the same time.
2. Separate her legs as you let her knees straighten.
3. Pull her legs back together.

Here is a song to go with the exercise (to the tune of "Here We Go Looby Loo"):

> *We bend our knees like this*
> *Now out to the side we go*
> *We snap our legs together again*
> *I love my baby so.*

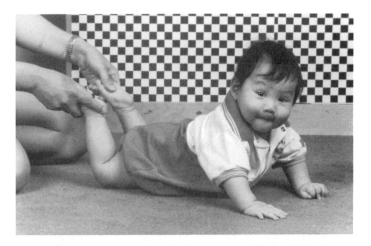

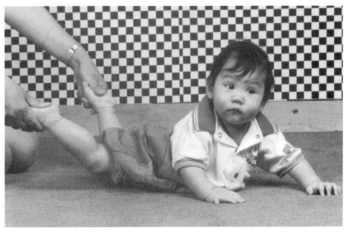

Quilt Roll

Spread a quilt on the grass and lay your baby on her stomach along one side of the quilt. Gently raise the quilt to help her roll from her stomach to her back. Reward her efforts with a kiss and a hug.

Hands Up

Move the baby's hands up and down, in and out, as you recite this jingle:

> *Up-up-up*
> *My baby goes*
> *Reach way up*
> *And touch your nose.*
> *Down-down-down*
> *My baby goes*
> *Reach way down*
> *Touch baby's toes.*

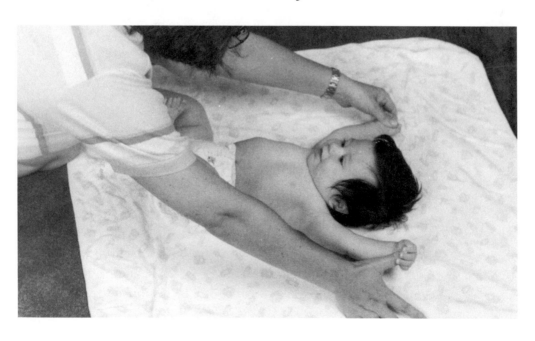

Out of Reach

If your baby has learned to move by squirming or crawling, place toys just out of her reach. She will discover that she has to both wiggle and reach in order to get the toy. Be careful not to frustrate her. If she doesn't reach the toy within a few seconds, put it within her reach.

The Wheels on the Bus

Lay your baby on her back. Sing this song while putting her through the indicated motions. Vary the pace of your song in response to your baby's

cues. While some babies enjoy a fast paced routine, most babies enjoy the song more if the pace
is slow and relaxed.

> *The wheels on the bus go round and round*
>   (roll baby's arms)
> *Round and round*
> *Round and round*
> *The wheels on the bus go round and round,*
>   *all over town.*
> *The people on the bus go up and down*
>   (baby's arms go up and down)
> *Up and down*
> *Up and down*
> *The people on the bus go up and down, all*
>   *over town.*
> *The wipers on the bus go swish, swish, swish*
>   (baby's arms go side to side)

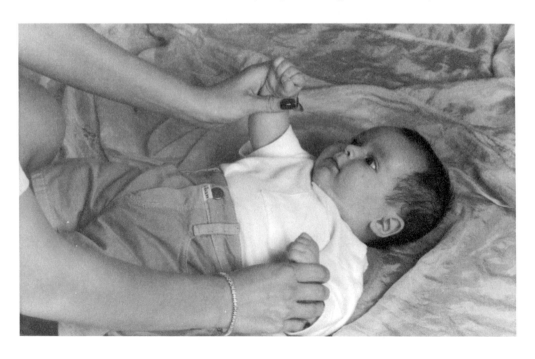

Swish, swish, swish
Swish, swish, swish
The wipers on the bus go swish, swish, swish,
    all over town.

Old Songs

Remember your baby enjoys the familiar as well as the new. Sing some songs from earlier months, such as, *"Here We Go, Up-up-up"* or *"Row, Row, Row Your Boat."*

SOLVING PROBLEMS

Two Timing

Give your baby two squeak toys, one for each hand. Make sure that they are made of soft latex so that your baby can squeak the toy with just one hand. Watch to see if she will look at the hand that is doing the squeaking. When she gets a little older, she will learn to make both toys squeak at the same time.

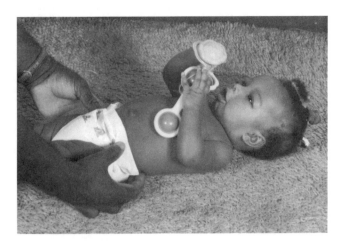

Scarf Bracelet

Attach a plastic bracelet to a colorful silk scarf, and tie the scarf around the arm of a chair. Your baby will grasp the ring and watch the scarf move up and down. Soon she will discover different ways to make the scarf move.

Curtain Ring Collision

Make a simple chain by attaching curtain rings together. Attach them to the side of the crib or on the back of a chair where your baby can make them swing. Your baby will discover that a big swing with her arms creates a collision and a delightful tinkling sound.

DAILY ROUTINES

Diaper Time/Bath Time

Double Rattles

Tie a ribbon around the center of each of two dumbbell rattles so that the rattles are about three inches apart. Let your baby hold on to one of the rattles. She will keep very busy trying to catch the other rattle while you change her diaper.

This Little Piggy

Your baby is discovering that she has feet. Help her become more aware of her body by playing this game before you dress her. Touch her toes one by one and end the song with a tickle.

This little piggy went to market
This little piggy went home
This little piggy had roast beef
This little piggy had none
This little piggy went whee whee whee all
the way home.

Finger Tip Play

Lightly run your fingertips across your baby's stomach while she is undressed on the changing table. Observe how she contracts her muscles in response. Turn her on her stomach and run your fingertip down her spine. She will arch her back and lift her head.

Baby Oil Rub

Your baby will enjoy having a massage after her bath. Although warm oil is most effective for a real massage, everything that you put on your baby's skin—soap, shampoo, diaper rash creams—can be applied in a massaging way that helps her relax.

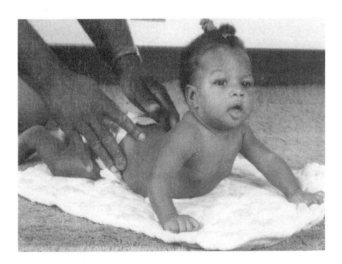

Mealtime

Spoon Reach

If your baby has begun eating solids, make sure she sees the spoon before it goes into her mouth. If she reaches for the spoon, let her hold it while you continue feeding her with another spoon.

Licking

Put a little drop of food on your baby's lips. As she tries to lick it off she is getting her tongue in shape for babbling.

Quiet Time

Huggie

Place a soft doll or stuffed animal in your baby's crib. Always use the same doll. Your baby will learn to associate the "huggie" with falling asleep.

Hammock Ride

Swinging in a hammock with your baby in your arms is wonderfully relaxing for both you and your baby.

Lullaby

Babies really enjoy the lulling rhythm of a lullaby. Sing the same lullaby for nap time and sleep time. Your baby will recognize the lullaby as a comforting sleep-time ritual.

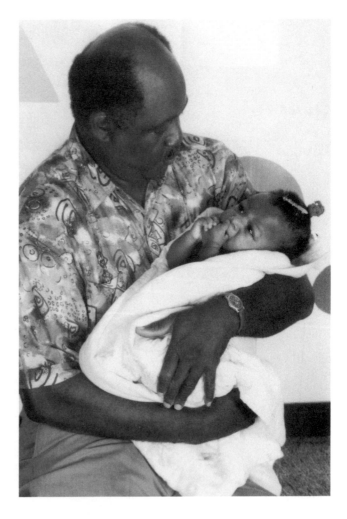

CHAPTER 6

FIVE MONTHS

Baby's Viewpoint

Your five-month-old keeps his hands busy during most of his waking hours. Not only can he scoop up a rattle or a ring, but he can also release it at will. If a toy happens to be out of his reach, he looks at it and opens and closes his hand in a kind of abbreviated, almost symbolic, movement. It is as if the rattle has developed a special meaning. "A rattle is something to grasp, to hold, and to shake." Your baby is trying to make sense out of his world. He has learned to define the things around him by what he can do with them.

Although your five-month-old warms up to strangers quite quickly, he makes a clear distinction between people he knows and people who are new to him. In a strange situation, your baby is likely to cling to a familiar person. When he is tired, hurt, or fussy, no one can soothe him as easily as you.

As you watch your baby's reactions to new people and new experiences, you will see that his emotional states are becoming more distinct. When your baby was younger his emotional repertoire included a continuum of emotions from happy to unhappy. Now, happiness appears in more distinct forms such as excitement, joyfulness, and quiet contentment; unhappiness includes wariness, sadness, and anger. Along with this increased repertoire of emotional states comes a new ability to use babbles to communicate feelings. Your baby can now send out babble messages that mean "look at me," "pick me up," and "I don't like it." Temperamental differences that you recognized when your baby was younger continue to influence his responses to new situations. A temperamentally sensitive baby will enjoy new experiences more if he is introduced to them slowly and gradually. On the other hand, a baby who is feisty will be enthusiastic about new experiences, but may suddenly tire and fall apart.

MOTOR SKILLS

Differences in the rate of motor skill development are quite apparent at five months old. While some five-month-olds are crawling efficiently around the house, others will not begin to crawl for several months. It is important to remember that accelerated motor development is not necessarily associated with greater intelligence.

Whether or not your five-month-old baby is crawling, he is likely to enjoy an activity that allows him to push with his feet. With your help, he may be able to push himself up to a standing position. A jump chair is especially popular. Babies love to push against the floor with their feet and bounce up and down. Make sure that the jump chair you use is strong and well balanced. A robust baby in an active moment can tip over a less than sturdy chair.

At five months, most babies are quite adept at reaching and grasping. They can grasp toys with one hand and then the other, and are quite good at lifting up their legs and playing with their feet. They have also learned to rotate their wrists in order to inspect the object they have grasped. This wrist rotation, combined with a new ability to use his thumb and fingers cooperatively, makes it easier for your baby to pick up small objects and even hold a spoon.

Your baby seems to realize now that there are two sides to his body. Some babies are able to hold a toy in one hand, transfer it to the other, and then change back again. As your baby looks from one hand to the other, or passes a rattle from hand to hand, he is just as interested in what his hands are doing as he is in the toy itself.

SEEING, HEARING, AND FEELING

Seeing plays a central role now in your baby's exploration of objects. At first, your baby batted at things because he wanted something exciting to happen again. Next, he used his grasping skill to get objects into his mouth. Now, at five months old, he appears to be grasping in order to play with an object. The rattle in his hand is twisted, turned, and carefully inspected before it finds its way into his mouth.

As your baby takes visual stock of his environment, he devotes particular attention to following your movements. When you step out of the room, your baby continues to gaze for a long time at the spot where you were. As you step back into the room, he follows every movement with his eyes.

At five months old, your baby will not only turn his head toward a sound, but will follow a sound in a darkened room. He is particularly sensitive to the sound of footsteps and becomes alert and attentive when he hears you enter the room. He continues to be interested in the sounds he can make, and he will experiment with different sounds. He may have discovered how to change his own sounds by babbling with a finger or a pacifier in his mouth. He loves to listen to music and often becomes more active when the music is rhythmic and lively.

At five months old, bath time may be one of the highlights of the day. By now, most babies have discovered how to splash and will start a splashing game as soon as they get in the water. This game usually involves batting the water with both hands. When he is really going at it, your baby will splash water in his own face and eyes, scream with surprise, and then go back to his splashing.

As well as providing your baby with an opportunity to splash, the bath is a good time for your baby to investigate his own body. Supported by your arms, your baby may be able to capture his toes. After playing for a while with his slippery toes, he is likely to discover his genitals. Then, during drying time, he may discover his navel, or content himself with a tactile investigation of his nose and ears. If your face is close enough he may inspect your face too, as if trying to make a comparison.

KNOWING YOUR BABY

Many five-month-olds begin to practice consonant sounds, like "ma-ma," "da-da," and "na-na." These early babbles are likely to be

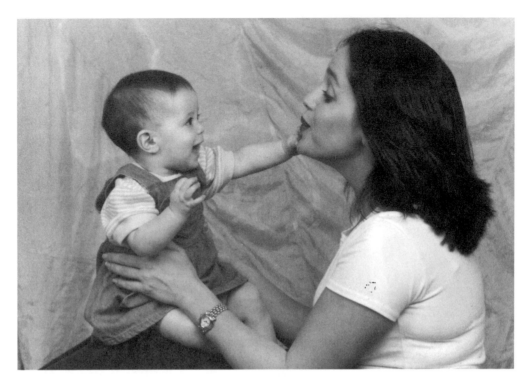

repetitive—"da-da" or "na-na" instead of just "da" or "na." Babbling sounds are catching. When your baby says "da-da" or "na-na," the rest of the family is likely to take up the chorus. Your baby responds to this enthusiasm by repeating those syllables over and over again. It is this sort of reinforcement that eventually turns babbling into talking.

Although a five-month-old baby does not associate any meaning with his babbles, even when they sound like words, he does learn to use language for his own purposes. He finds ways of calling his mother into the room and ways of bringing her back when she starts to turn away. By responding to your baby's call, you are teaching your baby the power of language.

When Mom or Dad return to the baby after a brief separation, a five-month-old welcomes their return with an array of greeting behaviors: waving his arms like a windmill, bouncing up and down, calling out with loud excited coos. Siblings and other familiar persons are also likely to receive a welcome, although it may not be quite so exuberant.

Between five and six months old, your baby may express his displeasure with the same intensity that he expresses delight. When your baby was younger, his expression of rage most often was a response to physical restraint. Now, at five months, your baby becomes enraged if he doesn't get what he wants. Taking away a toy, putting your baby down before he's quite asleep, or taking too long to put on a diaper can produce a strong expression of protest. Attach words to you child's emotional expressions. "You like the way your bath feels." "You're angry because you want your toy back." Of course, your baby is too young to understand your words, but he will understand at some level that you recognize and acknowledge his feelings.

Suggested Activities

SETTING THE STAGE

Touch-Me-Not Mobiles

Take down any remaining touch-me-not mobiles that your baby keeps trying to reach. Your baby is no longer contented with looking at interesting things. He wants to grasp, feel, twist, turn, and examine. If the mobile that your baby keeps reaching toward is not baby-proof, you are better off putting it away.

Baby Carriers

Baby slings that attach in front are better for taking baby out, because he can see your face when

you talk to him. While doing household chores, try carrying your baby on your back, papoose style.

Signaling

Tell your baby when you are going to pick him up, put him down, change his diaper, or place him in his bath or car seat. Your baby will learn that you are giving him a signal that a change is about to occur even before he can understand specific words.

Arm Stretch

Whenever you are about to pick up your baby, hold out your arms and say, "Up." After a while he will stretch his arms out toward you.

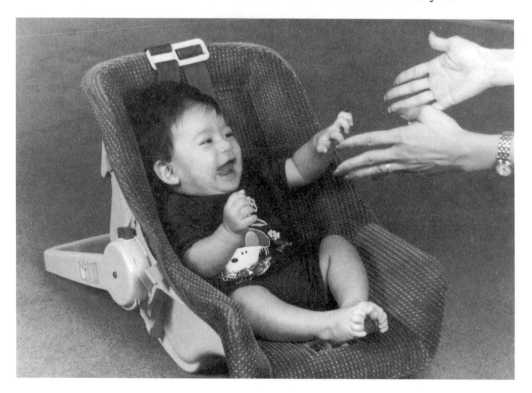

MAKING DISCOVERIES

Shiny Pan

Give your baby a large shiny pan he can see himself in. Let him pat it, roll it, bang it. Your baby loves to play with Mommy and Daddy's toys.

In the Mirror

Hold your baby up in front of a full-length mirror. He will love watching the baby in the mirror. An unbreakable mirror, hung next to the changing table, will make diapering time more interesting, as well.

Toy Treat

Keep a collection of small toys in the crib with your baby. Your baby will learn to tell his toys apart and will even choose a favorite toy or recognize a new toy that has been placed in his crib. When babies develop an early attachment to a favorite toy, whether it is a stuffed animal, a doll, or a blanket, it may become their faithful friend, providing comfort and security.

Roly-Poly

This is an ideal age for a roly-poly toy. Your baby's major interest now is making discoveries about interesting objects. A roly-poly doll, which rights itself when he knocks it over, is an excellent maintenance free toy that responds to your baby's actions.

Swing-a-Baby

Place your baby in an infant swing. As you push the swing away say, "Goodbye." As the swing comes back to you say, "Hello." Although your baby is too young to understand the words, he will recognize that you are using two different words. After a while he will be able to recognize that different sounding words have different meanings.

Touch That Sound

As your baby begins to experiment with his voice, you will notice several distinct sounds: "b," "m," "d," "ah," "ee," and "oo." It is fun to imitate. Place your baby's fingers on your lips while you make a sound. Let him feel the vibrations as each sound is made.

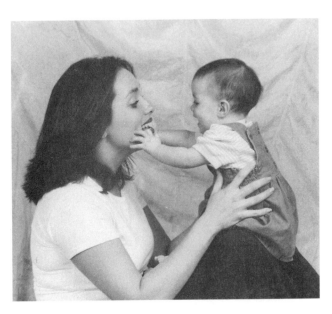

Toy Play

Encourage your baby to play with rattles and squeak toys. At first, he will play with all toys in the same way, mouthing, shaking, fingering, and watching as they move. When he is a little older he will discover that certain actions work best with certain toys: rattles are to shake, squeak toys are to squeeze, and pacifiers are especially good for sucking. Play with rattles helps him learn that rattles are good for shaking, and he will have fun practicing his shaking skill.

MOTOR SKILLS

How Big is Your Baby?

When your baby is sitting in the high chair or propped up in a sitting position, hold his hands down while you ask, "How big is your baby?"

Then, as you raise his arms over his head, add the words, "SO BIG!" If your baby responds with a laugh, you know he likes the game.

Bouncy Game

Babies enjoy a song or rhyme while being bounced on Mommy or Daddy's knee. Rhymes with a surprise ending are particularly fun. Your baby will learn to anticipate the ending activity and will let you know by smiling or laughing before the end comes. Try:

> *Baby be nimble, one, two, three*
> *Baby jump on my other knee.*

Ups-a-Daisy

Now that your baby has become adept at sit-ups (holding his head steady when you pull him to a sitting position), you might find that he is ready to try some beginning standing. You do have to remember, of course, that babies learn to straighten their knees before they learn to relax them. If your baby is ready to turn sit-ups into stand-ups, be sure to support your baby under the armpits. This way your baby can experience the fun of standing up without getting overtired.

Baby Roll

If your baby is learning to roll, make it easier for him to practice by taking him outdoors and placing his blanket on a slight incline.

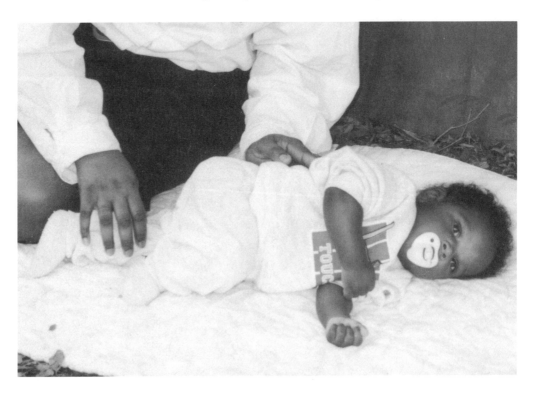

Tube Tumble

When your baby is learning to sit by himself, inflate a pool tube and put it around his waist. He will have the fun of sitting alone, and you will have the security of knowing that he won't get hurt if he topples.

One Hand—The Other Hand

Hand your baby a toy, first to one hand and then the other. Soon he will learn to transfer the toy from one hand to the other all by himself.

Face-Sheet

Faces continue to fascinate the five-month-old baby. Make a smiling face out of fabric or iron-on material. Sew or iron the face on the underside of his crib sheet. Your baby will lift up the sheet and discover the smiling face.

Ball Bounce

Bounce a large ball up and down while your baby is watching. He will get better and better at following the bounce with his eyes. Bounce the ball higher and lower, slower and faster.

Turnabout

Your baby can now tell the difference between a face that is drawn properly and a face that is distorted. Using a very sturdy paper plate, crayon a smiling face on one side, and a distorted face on the other side. (Put in extra eyes, or change the position of eyes and mouth.) Once your baby discovers the two faces he may attempt to turn over the plate. Which face does your baby enjoy looking at more?

Lost Ball

Roll a ball under a chair that is up against a wall, so that the ball hits the wall. See if your baby watches as the ball rolls back.

DAILY ROUTINES

Mealtime

Spoon Hold

Give your baby his own spoon during feeding time. He will be less likely to reach for your spoon. But don't expect him to feed himself. Just holding on to a spoon is an accomplishment in itself.

Cup Hold

Allow your baby to hold a cup. Some babies enjoy drinking from a cup at five months. There are many kinds of spill-proof cups on the market that reduce the amount of spilling.

Naming

As you dress or bathe your baby make up little rhymes about his eyes, nose, and mouth. Here is an example:

> *What a surprise,*
> *I'm washing your eyes*
> *And this I suppose, is a nose.*
> *And right under here, I've discovered an ear.*
> *But where, oh where, are your toes?*

Stone Face

In the middle of a diaper time conversation, stop talking and keep your face perfectly still. Observe your baby's efforts to get you going again.

Bath Boat

Placing boats in the bath with your baby will make bath time more fun. You can make an instant fleet out of plastic butter containers.

Quiet Time

Pat-the-Baby

When you feel that your baby is getting tired but can't quite settle down, hold him against your shoulder, rock back and forth, and pat him gently and rhythmically. He will relax along with you.

Hush-Hush

Whisper to your baby. He will enjoy the feeling of closeness.

Swaying

Babies love to sway back and forth while being held tightly in Mommy and Daddy's arms. Sing to your baby while you're swaying.

> *Brian is gently swaying, swaying, swaying,*
> * swaying*
> *Brian is gently swaying, swaying, swaying*
> *Swaying in the breeze.*

CHAPTER 7

SIX MONTHS

Baby's Viewpoint

When your baby is between six and seven months old, you may notice a subtle change in her behavior. Your nice, outgoing baby is becoming more fearful of new people. When a visitor approaches, her ready smile is not quite so ready. A familiar visitor may meet resistance when she tries to pick her up. Fortunately, your baby's initial shyness tends to be short-lived. A little time and a shared toy overcome the shyness, and before long the visitors are treated as welcome playmates.

Why does this subtle change take place? Has your baby really lost her easygoing disposition? Quite the reverse. Your baby's demonstrated preference for her parents is an overt expression of love. She has learned to associate Mommy and Daddy with safety, comfort, nurturance, and pleasure, and she does not want a substitute. A new person could signify a temporary separation from her parents.

Once your baby has gotten used to a new visitor, she is apt to be a very good entertainer. She is becoming aware of herself and her effect on other people. She will smile, wave her arms, kick her legs, and babble with gusto, as if she is saying, "Look at me." The more attention she gets from the visitor, the more likely she is to continue her performance.

MOTOR SKILLS

At six months, many babies have learned to sit up by themselves, with their hands planted firmly on the floor in front of them to help them hold their balance. This independent sitting gives them a new perspective on the world. It is a perfect age for grocery shopping. Sitting in the grocery cart baby seat, your baby is at the center of a new universe full of bright colors, clanging noises, and bustling activity.

During the seventh month many babies are becoming quite mobile. Some are scooting around on their stomachs, using legs as pushers and arms as pullers. Other babies may be creeping around on their hands and knees, with stomach well off the floor. On the other hand, some six-month-old babies who are also developmentally on target appear riveted to the floor. If you place a toy in front of them they strain to reach with their arms. Unsuccessful, they dig their feet into the carpet in an attempt to lurch forward. Unfortunately, these efforts are of no avail, and they end up further from their target than when they started. Often, we find that a baby who is especially well balanced in a sitting position will show no interest in crawling.

Grasp and reach are very precise now. Your baby can grasp a toy with either hand, transfer it from one hand to the other, and then reach out

with her empty hand to grasp a second toy. However, if you present her with a third toy when both hands are full, she may have a problem. She wants the new toy but doesn't realize that her hands are both full. In all probability, she will reach for the third toy and accidentally drop the second. It will take a while for your baby to learn how to put the second toy down in anticipation of picking up a third one.

Along with her increased efficiency in reaching out for objects, your baby is getting better at picking up small objects from the floor. Apparently, two things are happening. First, she is learning to use her thumb as well as her fingers to get a better hold on things. Second, she is learning to judge distance and can focus her eyes on a small spot. You are likely to see your baby struggle to pick up a crumb of bread, a piece of cotton, or even the design on the sheet.

At six months, many parents are interested in teaching their baby how to swim. The rationale is that swimming is like creeping and if a child is able to creep, she will be able to swim. Actually, whether the child is taught by a loving parent or a trained instructor, babies are able to hold their breath and paddle in the water for only a short distance. Few babies achieve the skill of lifting up their heads to take another breath and, with almost no exceptions, a six-month-old cannot swim purposefully from one spot to another.

Some parents or swimming instructors use a swim or sink approach. They feel that swimming is another form of crawling, and if young babies are put face down in the water they will swim. While this may be true for some babies, it can also induce a fear of water that is hard to overcome. On the other hand, babies who learn to swim and love it do not know that swimming alone is dangerous. A baby who is heading toward the pool can catch you off guard. This is particularly true as your baby becomes more mobile. Holding your baby securely in your arms while you pop up and down or walk through the water is the best swimming lesson you can give her.

SEEING, HEARING, AND FEELING

At six months, your baby is able to recognize many different sounds and sights. She pays attention to relatively small details and can tell the difference between a happy and a sad face. She enjoys playing with lots of different toys at the same time and particularly likes colored toys and toys that make interesting sounds. A ball with different textures, a soft rubber toy with a loud squeak, blocks with bells inside, keys, spoons, pots and pans, and brightly colored old-fashioned clothespins are favorite toys at this age.

Now that your baby can sit with support and grasp efficiently, her interest in playing with toys has reached a new peak. Although she tends to focus on only one toy at a time, she has learned a set of actions that she uses with each one. When she picks up a rattle, she is likely to start off her play by inspecting it with her eyes. A second or two later she shakes it vigorously, then fingers it with her other hand, bangs it against the floor, mouths it for moment, shakes it again, and then lets it drop. Moments later, she might pick up a toy with quite different properties and put it through a similar routine.

Your baby's interest in different sounds makes wrapping paper very exciting. She loves to crinkle tissue, wrapping paper, or mylar. Because her exploration might involve stuffing the paper in her mouth, her paper playing activities have to be carefully supervised. Don't let your baby put newspaper or magazines in her mouth. The ink contains a dye that could be harmful.

A major development at this age is the ability to recognize a familiar object when it is partly covered up. When a cloth is placed over her rattle so that it is partly hidden from view, your baby will reach for her toy with obvious excitement. It seems that she is getting closer to realizing that an object can exist, even when it is partially covered up. She still, however, is unlikely to search for her rattle if it is totally hidden. One explanation is that babies do not understand that objects continue to exist when they are not seen or felt. Another explanation is that babies do not realize that one object can be inside, underneath, or behind another.

KNOWING YOUR BABY

Your six-month-old is quite a sociable youngster despite her wariness of strangers. She loves to play with her sisters and brothers and visit other babies. When two six-month-old babies are put together, they notice and imitate each other. If one laughs, so does the other. If one cries, the other does, too. It seems as if your baby identifies with a playmate without really recognizing that her playmate is a baby like herself.

The mirror is now one of your baby's favorite toys. She will sit herself in front of a long mirror and talk to and even kiss her own reflection. When her image remains silent, she may pat the mirror as if trying to initiate a response.

As she gets better at holding images and sound patterns in her head, your baby's repertoire of back and forth games expands. She anticipates the climax of "I'm going to get you," and laughs out loud before the tickling begins. A version of peek-a-boo in which Dad peeks back and forth from behind a door can elicit peals of laughter. When you grow tired of a back and forth game and decide to end it, your baby may have a different idea. When you take a break from "Trot, trot, to Boston," your baby may bounce up and down to make the game continue.

Your baby's efforts to make an adult resume a game suggest that she is beginning to make some important distinctions between people and objects. She is discovering that people, but not objects, can make things happen. Your baby talks to toys in a conversational babble that does not require a response. The babble that is reserved for people is much more varied and interesting. It can sound like a question, an answer, a comment, or a command. If you attempt to put your baby down when she does not want to be put down, the ensuing babble is most definitely a command.

Your baby at six months old is learning to imitate the phrase patterns of the language that is spoken around her. Her babbling begins to sound recognizable even when it isn't. In a manner of speaking, the Chinese baby babbles in Chinese, the Cuban baby babbles in Spanish, the American baby babbles in English, and the hearing impaired baby loses interest in babbling.

Your baby also demonstrates a greater ability to imitate actions. Earlier imitation consisted mainly of facial expressions, vocalizations, and other aspects of communication. Now she is beginning to imitate your hand movements. This imitation is limited to copying actions that your baby already knows how to do. She also needs to see the part of her body that is doing the imitating. Your baby may clap her hands or bang on a pan when you model clapping or banging.

Suggested Activities

SETTING THE STAGE

Baby-Proofing

If your baby is learning to move around, baby-proofing is a necessity. Put gates across steps and staircases, close bathroom doors, plug up outlets, check for sharp corners, and place baby locks on cabinets. Remember, never take a chance! All poisons, cleaning fluids, and medicines must be kept out of reach. For further safety, keep the telephone numbers of emergency assistance, poison control, and your baby's pediatrician near your telephone.

Floor Play

Babies at this age need a lot of floor time to help develop crawling and creeping skills. If your baby doesn't enjoy being on the floor by herself, get down and play with her.

Basket Ball

Your baby may be beginning to take an interest in small toys and containers. Store her favorite things in a small basket and let her get things out herself. Several smaller baskets are preferable to one large toy chest.

Name Games

During the last few months, you mimicked the sounds your baby made and encouraged her to continue the cooing or babbling conversation. Now, at six months, you can take an even more active role in helping your baby tune into language. Play some naming games with your baby, like naming eyes, nose, hands, and toys.

Play Date

Invite another baby over to play with your baby. As babies look at, poke at, and investigate each other, they are making important distinctions between toys and real people.

MAKING DISCOVERIES

Pat-a-Cake

Play pat-a-cake with your baby over and over again.

> *Pat-a-cake, pat-a-cake Baker's man*
> *Bake me a cake as fast as you can*
> *Roll it, and knead it, and mark it with a "B"*
> *And put it in the oven for Baby and me.*

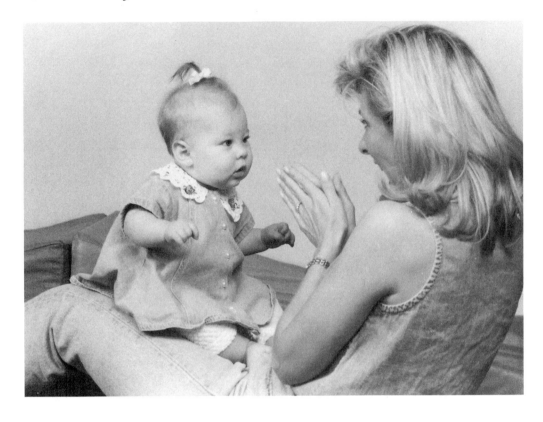

Cup Talk

Gather several empty cups in a variety of sizes. Place them in a shoe box. Talk into one cup at a time, repeating a familiar sound (e.g. your child's name). Your baby will notice how unusual her name sounds coming out of different cups.

Sound Game

Fill plastic bottles with different amounts of water. Tap the bottles with a spoon to produce different sounds. Your baby will notice the differences in sound. After a while she will join in the game.

Pin Ups

Name Mommy and Daddy at every opportunity. Place photos of yourselves close to your baby's crib or high chair. When she babbles "ma-ma" or "da-da," answer her by saying, "Here's mommy (or daddy)."

MOTOR SKILLS

Pop Goes the Weasel

Play Pop Goes the Weasel with your baby. Say the rhyme slowly. When you reach the "pop," raise your baby's arms high in the air. She will learn to anticipate the "pop" and will laugh when you reach the last line. (Be careful not to swing your baby by the arms or pull her arms up with a jerk. A baby's arms can be easily dislocated.)

Piggy-Back

Let your baby ride piggy-back on your shoulders as you hold her thighs firmly with both hands. This helps your baby develop balance and control and gives her a chance to look at the world from a different perspective.

Foot Ride

While sitting on a comfortable chair, give your baby an old-fashioned pony ride on your leg. Cross your legs and put her on your ankle. Hold her hands or place your hand under her arms. Lift your leg up and down as you sing:

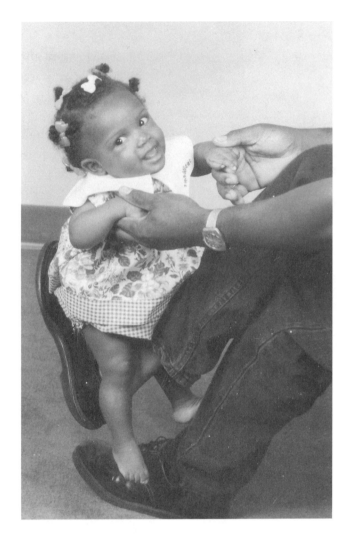

This is the way Amanda rides, Amanda rides,
*   Amanda rides* (ride slowly)
This is the way Amanda rides so early in the
*   morning.*

Repeat using "cowboys," and give baby a faster ride.

Obstacle Course

Make a simple obstacle course of different textured pillows for your baby to crawl across.

Roll and Crawl

Using a flutter ball is an excellent method for encouraging baby to crawl. Roll it slowly away from your baby. Verbally direct her attention to the ball. "Go get the ball. Hurry—get the ball."

Ball Play

Sit across from your baby as she sits in your spouse's lap. Roll the ball back and forth, singing:

I roll the ball to Baby
She rolls it back to me.

SOLVING PROBLEMS

Triple Challenge

Hand your baby a third toy when she has a toy in each hand. At first, she will try to grasp the third toy with her hands full. But with lots of practice, she will learn how to put one toy down before she grasps for a new one.

Toy Hide

Partially hide a favorite toy under a blanket or square of material. Your baby will learn to pull at the part of the toy she sees. When she is older, she will learn to remove the blanket before she reaches for the toy.

Car Slide

Slide a tiny car across a table so that your baby can watch it fall off. After a while she will anticipate the fall and look down on the floor before the car falls off.

Hide and Seek

Hide a wind-up radio under a diaper. Your baby will listen to the music and perhaps search for the box.

Pie Tin Fun

Give your baby two pie tins. Show her how to bang them together or bang them on the table.

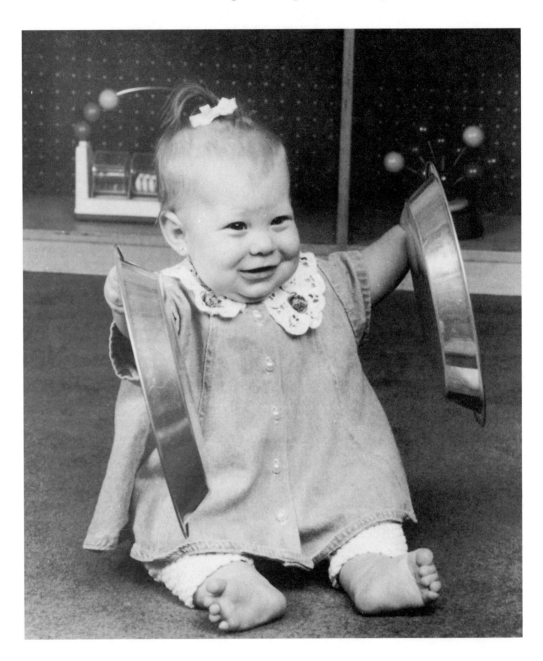

Balloon Pull

Tie a mylar or other non-breakable balloon to your baby's stroller with a wide ribbon. She will enjoy watching the balloon. After a while she might pull on the ribbon and watch the balloon move.

Busy Board

This is a good age to introduce your baby to a busy board. Choose one that has several items easy enough for small hands. Make sure the board is placed where it is accessible to your baby during playtime.

Bye-Bye

Waving bye-bye when you leave the room for a moment or two is a way to prepare your baby for longer departures.

DAILY ROUTINES

Mealtime

Pick Up

Six months is an age when many babies are able to sit comfortably in a high chair or baby chair during meal time. Help your baby develop finger dexterity by giving her small bits of food to pick up. For starters, try cereal-o's, slices of banana, or bits of unsalted crackers or tofu.

Suction Toys

Attach a suction cup toy to the high chair. There are a number of suction toys available that will stick to your baby's tray. Sitting still is easier when you have something to play with.

Big Bang

When your baby begins to bang on the high chair, try taking a turn and see if you can get a back-and-forth game going. Emphasize the word "bang" so she can learn to associate a word with an activity.

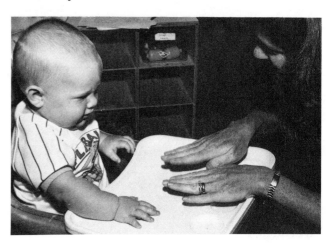

Straws

If you're eating at a fast food restaurant, use the straws and lids from drinking cups as an instant toy. Thread several lids on the straw, leaving some space between them. Show your baby how to pull the lids off the straw or make the lids spin.

Mello Jello

Let your baby experiment with texture by introducing her to "mello jello." Make small firm blocks of jello by using plain gelatin and fruit juices. Your baby will love to catch the jello as it squirms around on her tray.

Quiet Time

Happy-Sad Pillow

Make your baby a happy-sad pillow. Show her one side and then the other. This will help her notice differences in facial expressions.

Large Rag Doll

Give your baby a large rag doll and allow her to move the arms and legs up and down. Talk to your baby about what she is doing, using short sentences. You can also introduce your baby to the names of body parts. Say "head" as you point to the doll's head, or "toes" as you wiggle its toes.

CHAPTER 8

SEVEN MONTHS

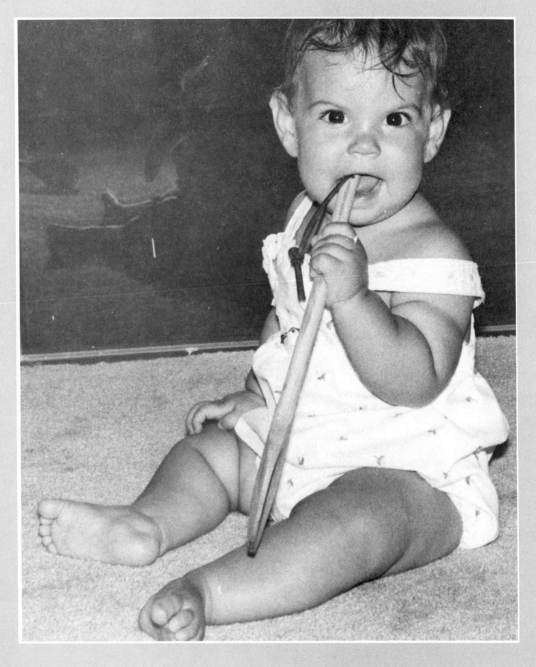

Baby's Viewpoint:

Whether he's sitting in the middle of the floor or crawling around, your seven-month-old baby is expanding his territory and quickening his pace. His toy play is more vigorous than it was a month ago. At one moment, he picks up a set of keys and puts them through their paces: shaking, banging, and waving them in the air; transferring them from one hand to the other; shoving them into his mouth. The next moment he picks up another toy and repeats the same routine. If someone approaches him during this play, he looks up for a minute or two and then returns to his game.

Your baby's extended investigation of an object and his ability to return to an activity after an interruption show an increased capacity to plan ahead and to hold an image in memory. At the same time, this foreshadows a new level of problem solving. As your baby plays with different objects, examining and comparing their properties, he makes the intuitive discovery that he can handle more than one object at a time. His thinking skills are expanding to match his widening field of exploration.

In some ways, your baby may not be as sociable as he was a few months ago. His enthusiastic greetings are reserved for people he knows well, and he may be wary of new people. This wariness does not mean that your baby is less friendly; he has just become more selective. You and your spouse are his very favorite people. You play with him, read his cues, and find ways to comfort him when he is out of sorts. When an unfamiliar person approaches, he tells you, without words, that he would rather be just with you.

MOTOR SKILLS

Most babies are able to sit alone at seven months old. They no longer need their hands for balance and can use them to reach, grasp, bang, shake, and poke. Crawling, too, is often achieved by this age. An active seven-month-old baby may take the next step and pull himself up to a standing position. Getting back down, of course, is another story. It is not unusual for a baby to pull up to a standing position, and then cry in panic until someone comes to pull him back down again. As these motor skills emerge, a baby's sleep may be more fitful. Even a good sleeper will awaken and attempt to crawl or pull up. It is as if your baby can't waste time sleeping with such important new skills to practice.

Your seven-month-old baby is busy practicing his ability to handle objects. He will play with a toy first with one hand and then with the other, with one hand mirroring what the other hand has just done. Even if a baby clearly uses one hand more often than the other, it doesn't mean that he is right-handed or left-handed. He may change preferred hands several times before you know for sure whether he is right- or left-handed.

SEEING, HEARING, AND FEELING

One of the most striking characteristics of the seven-month-old is his interest in visual detail. He notices the pattern on a new sheet and scratches the design with his fingers as if trying to pick it up. He is also becoming interested in the relationship of one object to another. He picks a block up in one hand, examines it with his eyes, picks up another block in the other hand, puts it through the same kind of examination, and then bangs the two together.

Your seven-month-old baby will also be intrigued with the orientation of objects in space. He can recognize a familiar object, such as a bottle or teddy bear, when it is upside down, and he is quite likely to turn it over. Curious about his own orientation in space, he squirms and wiggles in your arms, then throws back his head to see what things look like upside down.

Your baby is beginning to realize that one object can be on top of another, even if it looks like the two objects are one. For example, if a small object, like a poker chip, is placed on a larger object of similar shape, like a saucer, your baby may see that the poker chip can be picked up without moving the saucer.

Your baby may recognize that most objects have a front and back. Flat objects, such as books and pan lids, are flipped from front to back over and over again. Your baby may be trying to find out how these two different looking sides can be part of the same object. Round objects, which have no sides, are the most surprising of all. Your baby may rotate a round object several times as if trying to discover some sign of a corner, some indication that there is a front and back, or a top and bottom.

In the process of investigating objects, your baby discovers that some toys have moving parts and that other toys change shape. This intrigues him. He will catch hold of a string on a toy or the label of a stuffed toy and swing the toy around. He will spend as long as ten minutes crumpling a piece of mylar wrapping paper.

When your six-month-old baby searched for a rattle that was partly hidden under his blanket, he showed some understanding of object permanence. Now, at seven months, he has developed still another insight into the nature of objects. When he drops a toy off his feeding table, he looks down on the floor to see where it is. Remember, just a few months ago he continued to look in the place where he saw it last, expecting it to reappear. By looking to see where his toy has landed, your baby demonstrates his growing understanding that, when a rattle drops, it will fall to the floor and remain there unless someone picks it up.

Another sign of increased understanding is your baby's ability to go back to an activity that has been briefly interrupted. Your baby may be banging two blocks together when you enter the room. He'll stop and look at you for a moment and then go back to his banging. He remembers his blocks are there, despite the momentary distraction.

Peek-a-boo is a top favorite for the seven-to eight-month-old baby. It is another indication that your baby is learning that objects which disappear from sight are not necessarily gone forever. When you reappear from underneath a scarf, your baby's delighted laugh signals both his enjoyment of the game and his sense of relief. Although he guessed it all along, it's nice to know for sure that you are really still there.

KNOWING YOUR BABY

Your baby's vocabulary of sounds is increasing on a daily basis. Interestingly enough, many of the vowel sounds that he was practicing at two and three months old have been dropped. He is now more likely to practice a string of consonants. Often he discovers one particular babble and practices it for a week or so before going on to a new one.

Your baby enjoys listening to you talk and may be content to play alone for an hour or more if you talk to him from time to time. Your baby's ability to recognize his own name is a real forward step. He demonstrates this new learning by interrupting his play and looking toward the person calling his name. He is also learning to use gestures to control the people around him. If he wants his Dad to continue playing a game with him, he may yank at his Daddy's arm or bounce impatiently up and down. When he notices something interesting across the room and wants to share his discovery, he may point his hand in that direction and wiggle with excitement.

With familiar adults, your baby delights in using objects to play a back and forth social game. He hands a toy to Daddy, then puts out his hand to get it back. He finds a toy that is hidden in Mother's hand and returns it to her hand in order to replay the game. Your baby is creating a game with toys that parallels earlier parent-child conversations. He may even engage in such a game with a stranger, as long as the newcomer lets your baby do the approaching.

Despite this willingness to make new friends, your baby continues to be wary of strangers. He not only objects to the sudden appearance of a new face, but even when the stranger stays around for a while, his shy behavior may persist. Along with his increased ability to recognize an unfamiliar face comes a new sensitivity to changes in facial expression or tone of voice. When an adult tells your baby "no" in a sharp voice, he stops what he is doing, at least for a couple of seconds.

Suggested Activities

SETTING THE STAGE

Play Watch

Babies loves to watch other children at play. Give your baby opportunities to watch older children play. He will also enjoy a visit with a baby his own age.

Music Time

Babies respond differently to different kinds of music. Watch your baby. Does he move in rhythm to music with a strong beat, and relax and get sleepy with melodious music?

Name That Toy

Give your baby toys to play with that can be named easily: cup, telephone, doll, kitten, spoon, dog, block, rattle, banana, clown. Name each toy as he reaches for it.

MAKING DISCOVERIES

Picture Show

Cut out large pictures from magazines: a telephone, a dog, an airplane, a spoon, a teddy bear.

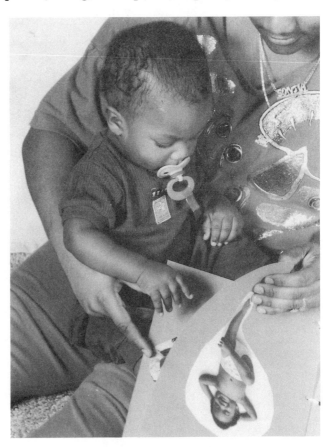

Paste the pictures over the pages of a pamphlet you were going to toss out. Now sit your baby on your lap and "read" about the pictures.

Bowl Drop

Now that your baby has mastered the skill of sitting, he can sit on the floor to play some dropping games. Dropping a hard ball into a large plastic bowl is a good activity to begin with. Hold your baby's hand over the bowl and encourage him to drop the ball. He will be intrigued by the sound of the ball bouncing in the can and will want to try again. After a while, he will drop the ball with just a little help.

Reflections

Help your baby explore mirror images. Show him a rag doll and then encourage him to look at the doll in the mirror. Watch to see if your baby looks back and forth between the real doll and its image.

Questions and Answers

Your baby is discovering in more and more ways that he can make things happen. Look for toys that respond to your baby's manipulations, such as busy boxes, squeak toys, pull toys, and pop-up toys.

MOTOR SKILLS

See-Saw Play

Try this familiar chant:

*See-saw, up and down, Baby is going to
    Baby's town.
See-saw, side to side, Baby is going for a ride.
See-saw, bumpty-bump, Baby is getting ready
    to jump.*

Tug of War

Have a tug of war with your baby. Give him one end of a scarf and pull gently on the other end. Your baby will enjoy this playful lesson in turn taking.

Punch Ball Fun

Hang a punch ball from the ceiling. Your baby will enjoy batting at it and watching it dance about.

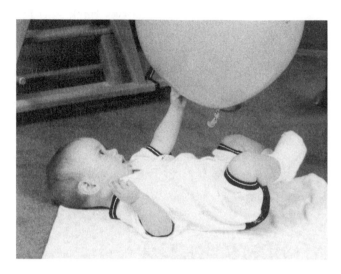

SOLVING PROBLEMS

Dancing Doll

Attach a ribbon to the head of a small rag doll or stuffed animal. Show your baby how to hold the toy by the ribbon in order to make it dance.

Squeak Toy Hide

Make one of your baby's toys squeak, hide it under a blanket while he is watching you, and then let him try to find it.

Small Ball Play

Give your baby several small rubber balls to pick up. Now that he is developing the ability

to pick up small things, he needs opportunities to practice.

Toy Bang

Bang two toys together. Then let your baby try it.

DAILY ROUTINES

Mealtime

Pick-Ups

With every meal, give your baby some food that he can pick up with his fingers, such as diced carrots, peas, bits of hamburger, or bits of unprocessed cheese.

Yogurt Paint

Put a dab of plain yogurt on your baby's tray and let him paint with his fingers.

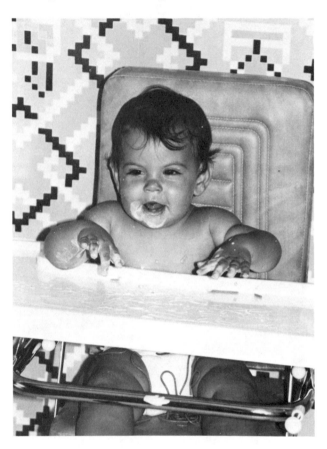

Bottle Hold

Try letting your baby hold his own bottle. If he objects, however, do not force the issue. Some babies are not ready for quite this much independence. Be sure you don't let your baby sleep with a bottle in his mouth. Babies who get into the habit of falling asleep with a bottle in their mouth may have trouble with their teeth.

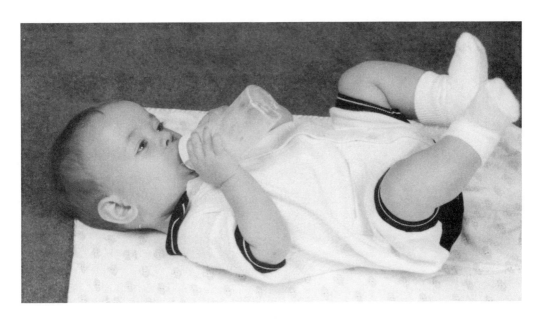

Spaghetti Challenge

Put some cool, cooked spaghetti on your baby's highchair tray. Playing with the slippery, wet noodles will delight your baby, and pulling apart the strands of spaghetti is a challenging game.

Bathtime

Flotilla

Put several different toys in your baby's bath. Talk with him about the toys he retrieves.

Back Stroke

Fill the bath tub with only two to three inches of water. Put your baby on his back and let him kick. Make sure to take him out of the bath if he doesn't enjoy this activity.

Diapering Toy

If your baby has started to squirm away at every diaper change, keep a special toy on the changing table to hand him as a distracter.

This is the Way

While bathing or diapering your baby, sing to the tune of "This is the way. . . ." (It is the same tune as "Here We Go Round The Mulberry Bush.")

> *This is the way we wash our toes, wash our*
>   *toes, wash our toes,*
> *This is the way we wash our toes so early*
>   *in the morning.*

Repeat, changing the words in succession to wash our face, change our diaper, kiss your tummy, say hello, etc.

Quiet Time

Light Switch Play

Let your baby help you turn off the light switch. Before you turn off the light, say, "Light's out." After a while your baby will make the connection between switching off the light and darkening the room.

Book Time

This is a good age to begin reading real books. Choose a baby book with sturdy pages and very vivid pictures (cloth books are more indestructible, but the pictures are not as bright). Sit your baby comfortably on your lap. As you turn the pages, name the picture and talk about it. "Look at baby. See the baby. Ooh! Touch the baby." End the activity before your baby gets squirmy.

You want your baby to associate reading with being happy, comfortable, and encircled with love.

CHAPTER 9

EIGHT MONTHS

Baby's Viewpoint

The eight-month-old baby is, in a way, a kind of enigma. On the one hand, she is becoming an adventuresome explorer, creeping away from her parents to investigate new territories. On the other hand, she is a timid soul shying away from strangers, afraid of new places, and resistant to going to sleep in an unfamiliar crib.

Actually, your baby's increased adventuresomeness and her timidity are both related to an increased awareness of her world. As your baby's memory span increases, she is able to distinguish between situations that are new and situations that are familiar. She knows that a foray into a new room is safe because she can keep in mind both the image of your face and the route back.

A new person, a new face, or a new bed is quite a different story. She cannot attach the new experience to anything familiar and cannot make a prediction as to what will happen next. All she knows is that the new person is not Mommy or Daddy, the new place has no familiar landmarks, and the new bed is not a place that's warm and safe for sleeping. She expresses her dismay with a scream, and if you arrive to find out what's wrong, she buries her head in the safety of your arm.

MOTOR SKILLS

A new accomplishment for some eight-month-old babies is the ability to climb up stairs. Once your baby has mastered the first couple of stairs the next ones are easier. Enthusiasm takes over, and up your baby goes to the top of the stairs. Getting back down the stairs is quite another matter. Fortunately, you are at hand to get her out of the predicament.

Parents solve the stair problem in many ways. Despite the inconvenience to other family members, the most common solution is a set of gates. Other parents are concerned about gates being left open accidentally and prefer to teach their baby a safe way to go down the stairs, such as turning on their tummy as they slide down. Of course, no solution is fool-proof and parents recognize that their baby's only real safeguard is a watchful adult.

Even if there are no stairs to worry about, being the parent of an active eight-month-old requires constant vigilance. The baby who is trying to pull up and stand may pull on lamp cords, plant leaves, tablecloths, virtually anything she can reach. Pieces of furniture that tip are particularly dangerous. Your baby has little knowledge of stability.

A baby at eight months is quite adept at using her thumb and fingers to pick up small bits

of food. Because she can move around and get into new places, it is particularly important to keep beads, buttons, and other small objects away from your baby. Things that get picked up are still quite likely to find their way to your baby's mouth.

Your eight-month-old demonstrates her knowledge of a familiar environment by navigating through it. As she creeps around the house, she finds her way around tables and chairs, backs out of closets, and ducks her head when she finds herself under a low bed. To some degree she can tell the difference between a spot that is safe and a spot that is dangerous and is not too likely to fall off the end of a bed or roll off the changing table. Of course, the very fact that your baby is careful most of the time makes it doubly important for you to stay on guard.

SEEING, HEARING, AND FEELING

At seven months old, your baby was especially attracted to toys that had labels, handles, strings, or any easy-to-grab parts. Although this interest continues at eight months, your baby's fascination is with toys that either come apart or somehow fit into each other. She is just becoming aware of containers and is delighted by her daily discoveries of new kinds of containers: pots with dirt, dog dishes with water, mouths with teeth, boxes with tissues, and purses full of all kinds of delightful things. Now, her greatest joy is in emptying containers, but within a few months emptying drawers and cupboards and filling them up and emptying them again becomes a favorite activity.

As your baby empties containers and investigates their contents, she is continuing her self

study on the properties of objects. One of the major concepts that your baby is grappling with is the idea that objects exist even when you can't see them. With actions rather than words, your baby keeps asking the question, "Will the set of keys that just fell into a plastic bucket still be there when I reach inside?" By the age of eight months she can solve the mystery of a disappearing object if the object is hidden in an obvious way. A teddy bear that is totally covered with a blanket can be uncovered; a toy that disappears into Dad's shirt pocket can be fished out. Each of these experiences helps your baby learn that objects are permanent. Her teddy bear is still there, even when she cannot see it.

The most important permanent object in your baby's life is you, and she has learned from months of experience that when you go away you come back. She knows, for example, that if you pick up your purse or your briefcase, or put the leash on the dog, you are about to leave. She also is aware of the signs that mean you are coming back, the sound of your car in the driveway, or the sound of the key in the door. The enthusiastic greeting you get lets you know how happy she is to see you again.

When your baby is inside the house, she is likely to expend a great deal of energy keeping track of you. You cannot always be in a place where your baby can see you. You may have to answer the telephone or attend to a household chore. Your eight-month-old may call out anxiously when you leave the room, and regain her composure when you answer her call. A baby who has mastered creeping may leave you voluntarily and venture into another room. As your baby discovers her own ability to leave and come back, she is confirming her belief that people and other objects continue to exist when they are out of her sight.

Peek-a-boo and hide-and-seek games, which are related to a baby's discovery of object permanence, continue to be charged with excitement. In a favorite version of peek-a-boo, Mother hides her head under the blanket, and baby shrieks with delight as she pulls the blanket away. It is as if your baby is saying, "Look what I just did. I made my Mommy come back."

Every day, in the course of her active investigations, your eight-month-old comes across new questions to ask and new problems to solve. She hears an airplane sound and looks up in the sky. She tries to touch the sound inside a music box. She wonders how she can reach the goldfish when her hand won't go through the glass. What will happen if she pulls on the string of a pull toy, her big sister's hair, or the corner of the cloth on the dining room table?

KNOWING YOUR BABY

At eight months, your baby's babbling includes almost all the sounds of her language. Talking on a toy telephone is apt to be a favorite game. Some babies prefer the real telephone, while others seem frightened when a familiar voice that usually comes from Daddy's mouth is all of a sudden inside the phone.

Although your eight-month-old has not mastered meaningful words, she is quite adept at using babble messages to communicate her intentions. "Dadada" is likely to be an invitation to play. A whiny "mamama" may mean, "I need some cuddling." A high pitched string of vowels may mean, "Don't you go out of this room, I want you here." The eight-month-old is also sensitive to tone of voice. Without knowing what you are saying, she knows full well when you are pleased, excited, cross, or indifferent.

Handing a toy back and forth is still a fun way to play with adults, but now some new object games are appearing. Your baby enjoys a game of ball according to her own rules. She retrieves the ball that you throw across the room and expects you to retrieve the ball that she releases. Another version of the game involves sweeping all the toys off the high chair and watching you pick them up. Parents, of course, get tired of the game long before their baby does.

Your eight-month-old is receptive to imitative games. You and your baby can take turns patting a squeak doll, banging a pot, drinking from a cup, putting a hat on your head. Now your baby may be able to imitate an activity even when she can't see the part of her that is doing the imitating. This new skill is associated both with her improved visual memory and her recognition that things can still be there even when she doesn't see them.

Suggested Activities

~~~~~~~~~~~~~~~~~~~~~~~~~~~~~~~~~~~~

INTRODUCTION

Throughout *Your Child at Play* we emphasize the importance of observing your baby and letting him be the leader. For many babies, eight months old is a time of transition. Your baby is showing you how much she needs you and how much she loves you. At the same time, she has her own agenda. She knows what toy she wants to play with, and she will go after it. She knows what skills she wants to master, and she will practice these skills over and over again. She knows what people she wants to interact with and makes her preferences very clear. Our play ideas are only suggestions. Let your baby be your guide.

SETTING THE STAGE

Now that your baby is on the go and can explore many parts of the house, make her world interesting (and safe!). Give your baby her own cabinet in the kitchen filled with containers and spoons. A special drawer in the bathroom will keep your baby busy as you get ready to go out. Fill the drawer with paper towel spindles, interesting boxes, books, or toys. Small baskets of toys kept in different rooms give your baby something new and exciting to play with as she moves through the house.

Take advantage of your baby's increased interest in language. Carry on a running commentary about things you and your baby are doing. Talk to your baby in short but complete sentences.

Library Holdings

There are a number of books that babies love at this age. Activity books such as *Pat the Bunny* and *Telephone* are perennial favorites. Let your baby read a variety of books: books with one picture on each page so she can learn new words, books with more detailed pictures so she can search for a special friend or favorite object, and books with short rhymes that accompany the pictures.

MAKING DISCOVERIES

Visit! Visit! Visit!

Your baby is very aware of other people at this age. She loves talking to both grown-ups and children. It is also an age where some babies become fearful of strangers. As you provide your baby with opportunities to be around other people, she will become less wary.

Telephone Games

Encourage your baby to talk. Let her play with a toy phone, or, better yet, disconnect your phone and give her the real thing.

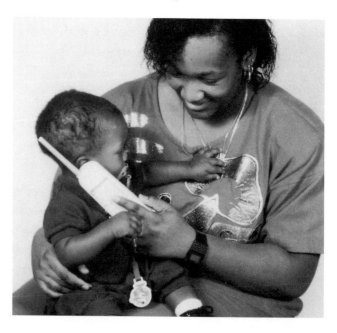

Sound Search

Call your baby's attention to different sounds by naming the source of the sound: the telephone, door bell, Daddy's footsteps, rain, running water, a barking dog. Even though your baby is unlikely to understand your words, she will learn to pay attention to different sounds and try to find out where they come from.

Hat Game

Give your baby a hat that she can put on her head. As she tries to reach for the hat, she is learning more about herself. Try the game with different kinds of hats, or even a bowl. Let your baby admire herself in the mirror.

Outdoor Noises

Take your baby outside in a carriage or stroller. When you see a bird, hear an airplane, or notice a dog approach, share your baby's excitement. Point with your finger and say, "Airplane, airplane, see the airplane." When your baby is a little older, she will learn to look in the direction of your pointing and will associate words with interesting objects that move.

The Dog Says, "Woof"

Babies are drawn to animals. Get your baby a set of plastic animals and show her the noise each one makes. "The dog says woof, woof. Can you find the dog?"

Oatmeal Pie

When your baby is sitting out in the grass, put raw oatmeal in a pie tin. She will enjoy mixing it with her hand or feeling the oatmeal slide through her fingers.

MOTOR SKILLS

Row-Row-Row

Do sit-ups with your baby as you sing, "Row-row-row your boat, gently down the stream; merrily, merrily, merrily, merrily, life is but a dream." Vary the pace. Sing the song fast and then slow, loud and then soft. Sway your baby from side to side as well as up and down.

Crawling Over, Under, and Through

As your baby is creeping and cruising and eventually walking, she is discovering some new facts about the size of her body and the objects in her world. What will she fit under? What can she crawl over? How far can she reach? The more experience of this kind she has, the more she becomes aware of the size of her body and the amount of space her body takes up. You can provide your baby with some of these experiences by encouraging her to crawl through a tunnel, under a table, or over a mound of pillows.

Wheelbarrow Walk

With your baby lying on her stomach, lift her legs two or three inches from the floor. While she supports herself on her arms, encourage her to walk forward.

Hiding Games

Crawling babies love hiding and chase games. Hide behind a chair and call to your baby so she can find you. Give your baby a turn to hide.

Baby Swinging

Swing your baby in your arms or on a swing, or ride her up and down on your knee. These games help your baby develop balance and control.

Climb and Fetch

If stairs are available, use them to help your baby exercise. Place a toy at a higher stair than your baby. Climbing up the stairs is a task most babies thoroughly enjoy.

SOLVING PROBLEMS

Follow the Leader

Play "follow the leader" games with your baby. Bang a drum, knock, clap your hands, wave, blow, lead an orchestra. See if she copies your actions.

Big Bang

Give your baby a wooden spoon and show her how to bang. Give her different surfaces to bang: a flat cookie pan, a place mat, a magazine. Your baby will enjoy the banging and will recognize differences in sound and feel.

Block Tower Play

Build a tower of blocks for your baby. Show her how to knock it down. As the tower crashes use words such as, "Uh oh, it all fell down." Your baby will soon delight in her ability to produce such an outstanding effect.

Blanket Pull

When your baby is on your lap, sitting at the table, place a toy on a place mat out of your baby's reach. She will have to pull the mat in order to retrieve the toy. Her ability to accomplish this game signals a new level of understanding. Your baby recognizes that one object can rest on another. If you hold the toy a little above the place mat and your baby still pulls it, you know she has not quite mastered the concept.

Upside Down Cup

Place a cup with a handle upside down on a table. See if your baby can grasp the handle and turn the cup upright. If she practices this task she is discovering the difference between right side up and upside down.

Toy Hide

Hide a toy under a blanket while your baby is watching. Let her lift up the blanket and find her toy. Because she is just learning that objects can be present even though they are covered up, there is an element of surprise in this game that adds to the fun of playing.

Pots and Pans

Pots and pans are more fun than any store-bought toy, particularly if they are shiny. Show your baby how to put a lid on a pan (her first puzzle). As she gets more accomplished, give her two different size pans with lids and see if she can figure out which lid goes with each pot. It's also fun to hide things in the pots and let your baby take off the lids to find her surprise. If you don't mind a little noise, show her how to bang the lids together.

Home-Made Toy Box

Using a large cardboard box to store your baby's toys is not only useful but it may provide an interesting challenge. Cut a large shape out of each side. Cover with interesting contact paper. Place her toys inside and let her figure out how to get them out.

Balls in a Bowl

A large bowl with a rounded bottom provides your baby with a new challenge. She must hold the bowl with one hand and place the balls in the bowl with the other hand. The unstable bottom makes the activity more fun.

Muffin Tins

A muffin pan with tennis balls is fun to play with. Your baby will experiment by putting the balls in the holes.

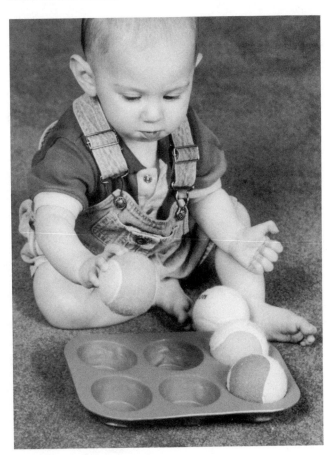

Barrier Challenge

Now that your baby is learning about hiding games, play games where you hide a toy behind a barrier. Put a toy behind a lucite tray or a see-through picture frame. Will your baby reach for the toy directly or will she reach around to get the toy?

Cereal Spill

Place some cereal-o's in a plastic bottle. See if your baby can figure out how to tip over the bottle to get hold of the cereal-o's.

Find the Picture

Put an interesting picture on one side of a carton and turn the carton around as your baby watches. See if your baby will crawl around the carton until she discovers the picture.

Egg Carton Game

Place plastic eggs in an egg carton and some outside the carton. Does she take some eggs out of the carton? Does she keep putting them back until the carton is full?

Bouncing Baby

Put on the radio or play a tape and then hold your baby in a standing position. She will love bouncing up and down as she listens to the music.

DAILY ROUTINES

Mealtime

Juice Pops

If your baby is having trouble with teething, make popsicles out of juice diluted with water. (Many companies sell popsicle-making sets with plastic handles.) She will enjoy licking her popsicle and helping you hold the stick. A frozen banana works well with some babies.

Restaurant Play

Keep your baby busy while you sit in a restaurant by showing her how to roll a small car across the tray of her high chair, or letting her play with an ice cube.

Bathtime and Diaper Time

Twinkle Twinkle

Sing this silly song or make up one of your own (to the tune of "Twinkle Twinkle Little Star"):

Twinkle twinkle little eyes
You're so little and so wise
Wash your ears and wash your nose
Washing you from tip to toes
Twinkle twinkle baby mine
Now you're scrubbed up clean and fine.

Butter Boat Play

Make your own bath toy by using butter tubs for boats and placing a red rubber ball inside. Initially, your baby will enjoy watching the ball in its boat. Before long, she will attempt to catch it.

Toe Hunt

Tie a bright ribbon to your baby's toe when you put her in the tub. She will have fun trying to pull it off.

Wash Up

Give your baby her own wash cloth. After a while, she will make some beginning attempts to wash parts of her body.

Quiet Time

Pat Pictures

Make a "pat" book for your baby, pasting different materials on each page. Cotton squares, satins, rubber carpet ends, velvets, and corduroy all produce interesting sensations. "Read" the pat book with your baby before she falls asleep by letting her feel the material as you turn each page.

Smelly Stuff

Add interesting scents to fabrics. Rose or lavender essence, perfume, shaving lotion, or a drop of vanilla will add another sensory dimension. Don't continue the activity is your baby is resistant or disinterested. Some babies do not like strong smells.

Photo Watch

Glue a photo or make a large picture of a baby on a sheet of cardboard. Place a cloth over the picture. Now play a new game of peek-a-boo. "Where is the baby? Here she is! You found the baby! Good night baby. It's sleep time." Pat the picture as you say good night.

Window Watch

Hold your baby near the window in the evening. Looking out at the darkness has a calming effect.

CHAPTER 10

NINE MONTHS

Baby's Viewpoint

As babies progress through the first year of life, individual differences both in the pace of development and in leading skills make it increasingly difficult to state precisely at what age a developmental milestone occurs. Remember, when we talk about the nine-month-old we are really talking about many, but not all, nine-month-olds. The one constant is the sequence of development within a particular domain. A baby, for instance, will learn to stand before he walks, or to scoop an object into his hand before he picks it up with thumb and finger.

Regardless of developmental status, your nine-month-old baby is likely to show an interesting change in the pace of his activity. Whether he is practicing his ability to get around the house, or playing with toys, his rate of exploration is speeding up. Day by day, he becomes noticeably more vigorous and his skills more proficient. At around nine months old, your baby also demonstrates a better memory for past events and an increased ability to solve simple problems. If you try to give him a spoonful of baby food that he rejected earlier, he will push it forcefully away. If you slip a toy inside his sweater, he will pull up the sweater and let it fall out. Quite obviously, he is reaching a point where he can direct his efforts toward a well-defined goal.

Nine months is an especially delightful age. Your baby is not only active, playful, and excited about learning, he is also cuddly and affectionate. He tells you in gestures, expressions, and strings of babbles that you are the most important person in his life. As you uncode his non-verbal messages, join his play, and provide hugs and cuddles, you are letting him know that he can always trust you to be there when he needs you.

MOTOR SKILLS

By nine months old, most babies have a well developed style of creeping. Hands and knees creeping, which allows babies to climb over obstacles and maneuver on different surfaces, is certainly the most common. Some babies, however, will slide along on their rear ends, some will hop forward using one leg as a pusher, some will pull themselves along the floor with their arms, and others will creep straight-kneed like a wobbly colt.

While many babies at nine months are developing new motor skills—standing, cruising, climbing up stairs, sliding off sofas—others seem to be at a standstill. All babies have peaks and plateaus in their development. They learn quite rapidly for awhile, and then need time to practice and consolidate before going on to new things. Often, however, when your baby appears not to be progressing in one area of development, he is making important gains in another area.

Nine months is an important age for developing small muscle and large muscle skills. While some babies spend much of their time getting ready to walk, other babies are more intent on manipulating small objects. Spoons may take on special significance. Babies learn that a spoon not only serves as a drumstick, it can also be used as a tool for bringing food to your mouth. Although your baby may turn the spoon upside down before it reaches his mouth, he will grasp the idea of first putting food on the spoon and then putting the spoon in his mouth.

SEEING, HEARING, AND FEELING

Many babies at nine months will search selectively for a favorite toy or blanket. A dirty teddy bear tossed in with the morning wash can start a family crisis. Despite the potential problems the favorite toy creates, this early object attachment is an important developmental event. It shows that your baby can make fine distinctions—a substitute teddy is rejected forcefully—and can remember what a toy looks like even when it is out of sight.

Your baby's ability to make fine discriminations is as noticeable with sounds as it is with sights. He is particularly attentive to sounds that allow him to anticipate the events of the day— the buzz of a razor means Daddy is awake, the closing of the refrigerator door means breakfast is ready, the patter on the window means rain.

As well as making more meaningful discriminations, your baby is becoming more adept at planning ahead. This planning ability is especially evident when he is presented with a two-step problem. If his favorite truck is stuck behind another toy, he will push the obstacle aside to get the truck. If you slide a plant to the other side of the coffee table out of your baby's

reach, he will cruise around the coffee table in order to touch the plant. In these situations, your baby is demonstrating an ability to coordinate two actions. In effect, he is using one act as a means of accomplishing another.

The same kind of advanced planning is reflected in the way your baby handles familiar objects. Just two months ago he was putting every object he picked up through the same set of experiments: examining, shaking, banging, and mouthing. Now, when your baby picks up an object, the actions he performs tend to take into account the special properties of the object. He shakes a rattle because that is what rattles are for. He puts a cup to his mouth, he crinkles a piece of mylar paper, he rings a bell. It is as if your baby has a different goal in mind with each object and the actions he performs are a means of achieving that goal.

Emptying is another goal-oriented activity that becomes more prominent at nine months. Your baby places a toy in a box, tips the box over, picks up the toy, and places it back in the box. We can look at this kind of repetitive activity as a version of hide and seek. He is investigating whether or not the toy still exists when it is hidden in the box.

Now that your baby is more sure about object permanence, hide and seek games appear in a whole variety of forms. If you close a toy inside your hand, he will pry it open. He initiates his own games, opening up the kitchen cabinets, pulling out the pots and pans, and distributing them around the house. This game, of course, will go on for many months.

KNOWING YOUR BABY

At nine months old, your baby shows an emerging ability to attend to and respond to words. He will look from one parent to the other in response to "Where's Mommy?" "Where's Daddy?" He will give Mommy a spoon in answer to a simple command, especially if Mommy communicates what she wants by holding out her hand. He also is more apt to understand a verbal command, such as "Give Mommy the spoon," if he is looking at the spoon when Mother makes the request. Once he has achieved success with this kind of game, he will enjoy playing it over and over again.

As your baby discovers the connection between people and their names, he begins to babble with gusto when a familiar person appears. Quite by chance your baby may say, "Da, da, da," when Dad appears. A few minutes later, he will babble, "Da, da," with the same enthusiasm when Mother comes into the room.

Back and forth games continue to be popular. One of the most popular, from the point of view of the babies at least, is pulling a parent's glasses off. Almost as popular is the "I'm going to bite you" game, where your baby sticks his hand in Daddy's mouth, Daddy bites down, and baby withdraws his hand and grins victoriously. A variation of the game is "I'm going to get you," when Mommy charges at baby's tummy and baby blocks the charge.

A somewhat calmer back and forth game is telephone. Using a toy telephone or the real phone with the plug pulled out, you and your baby each take a turn talking into the phone. You make a ringing sound, and then talk into the phone, "Hello, how are you? Are you eating lunch?" Then Mom or Dad hands the phone to baby, saying, "Now it's your turn." After a while, your baby learns to babble into the phone before trying to put the receiver back in its cradle.

When babies have had a lot of experience with different peers, or have become very familiar with one peer, we may see the same kind of turn taking, although perhaps in a more primitive form. Your baby hands a stuffed animal to a peer, the peer shoves the animal away, and your baby repeats the offer. The fact that both babies are smiling lets you know that you are watching a turn-taking game.

Suggested Activities

SETTING THE STAGE

The nine-month-old baby does not take "no" very seriously, and the whole house is fair game from his point of view. Recognizing his need to explore and manipulate, it is time to take another baby-proofing tour of your house. Any room that your baby may be in either alone or when you are busy must be gone through with a fine tooth comb. You need to think about, not only what your baby can do now, but what he will be learning to do in the next month. What cabinets and drawers will he open? What lamp cords will he pull on? What ornaments will he investigate and send smashing to the floor?

As you tour your house seeking out danger spots, you need to think about safe things for your baby to play with. Make sure that every room where you and your baby may spend time together has a cache of toys or items that can be played with. Parents often reserve one low cabinet in the kitchen, one drawer in their own bedroom, and one basket in the living room for non-destructive, safe items.

Take time to sit down and play with your baby. Sometimes he will initiate a game. At other times, you can take the lead. Placing a basket of new and interesting items within your baby's reach, such as a set of keys, some film cans, some dried fruits, and some hair rollers, can inspire your baby to begin a game of passing back and forth.

MAKING DISCOVERIES

Bell Ring

Give your baby a toy bell and show him how to ring it.

Feely Game

Give your baby his own box of "feel" materials. Make sure that it includes rough materials as well as smooth ones. A good collection of feel items might include a linoleum square, a playing card, a large rubber sink stopper, a square of velvet or satin fabric, and a sponge. Cut the board-

ers of the fabrics with pinking shears so they won't ravel. As your baby empties and fills his feel box, he learns to distinguish different textures.

Upside Down Toys

Turn toys upside down and put them in front of baby. (Teddy bear standing on his head, etc.) Encourage him to turn the toys right side up.

Sticky Stuff

Put a piece of scotch tape on the back of your baby's hand. Pulling it off will be an interesting challenge.

Hat Show

Put a hat on your baby's head when he is sitting in front of a mirror. He will enjoy watching his reflection as he pulls the hat off his head.

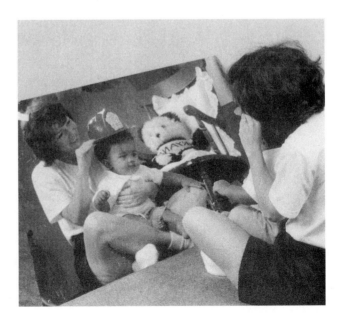

MOTOR SKILLS

Hand-Clapping Game

Play a hand-clapping game with your baby. Clap his hands together and then hide them under a blanket. He will love watching his hands go away and come back.

Clap your hands, one-two-three
Play a clapping game with me.
Now your hands have gone away,
Find your hands so we can play.

Ball Roll

Roll a ball back and forth with your baby. Let the family join the game. A soft fabric ball works well.

Sit Downs

If your baby is in that in-between stage where he can pull himself up but can't figure out how to get back down, let him practice holding on to the end of a towel or broom handle while you hold the other end. You can ease him back down to a sitting position.

SOLVING PROBLEMS

Spindle Toy

Give your baby a spindle toy with a large cloth or plastic donut ring. Once he has learned to place the ring on the spindle, he will practice again

and again. Add an extra challenge by using a spindle that rocks.

See-through Box

Put some of your baby's toys in a plastic see-through shoebox. Let him try to take the cover off himself. If he has trouble, take the cover half off for him.

Toy Drop

Give your baby a pile of very large wooden beads and a plastic bowl. Show him how to drop the beads into the container. After a while, he will learn how to reach in and get the beads.

Upside Down Fun

Hand your baby a pot upside down. See if he will turn it over. Your baby may begin to discover the difference between right side up and upside down.

Give Me the Toy

Place three different toys in a box. Name one of the toys and ask your baby to hand it to you. If he gets it wrong, name the toy he gave you. If he gets it right, say "Yes, that's a . . ."

Scarf Pull

Tie several colorful scarves together. Insert one end into a cardboard tube. Let your baby pull the scarves through the tube. Now, try a new problem: can he stuff the scarves back into the tube?

DAILY ROUTINES

Mealtime

Teddy's Mealtime

When your baby is learning to use a cup, give his teddy an occasional sip. Perhaps your baby will copy what you are doing. This early game of let's pretend is a forerunner of later imaginative play.

Food for Thought

Cooking is interesting for children of all ages, and even a baby can be involved in preparations. Give your baby a pot, lid, and spoon. As you empty a box or container, give it to your baby. He will enjoy imitating by holding the rice box over the pot, then stirring and banging.

Diapering Time

Diaper Duet

Your active nine-month-old can make diapering a challenge. It is usually easier to catch your baby on the run rather than placing him on the changing table. Speed up the routine by singing a special ditty when you change his diapers.

Zip—zip zip—off it goes
I see baby without clothes
Zip—zip—What do I see?
Diaper goes on with a one-two-three

Catch a Baby

Another way to meet the diapering challenge is to join in the fun! As your baby tries to escape, catch his legs and pull him back. "I've got you!" Playing this game several times will tire your baby at least long enough for you to change him.

Powder Puff

While your baby is being changed, he might enjoy a clean powder puff or cotton ball to explore. Show him how to rub it on his tummy,

arms, nose, or face. Not only will he be still for the change, but he will also learn about the different parts of his body.

Eensy Weensy Spider

That familiar old tune becomes new if you let the spider walk up your baby's leg, and around his tummy. It isn't nearly as hard for your baby to stay still if he is enjoying a game.

Bathtime

Dry Up

Give your baby his own towel. Encourage him to try drying himself.

Kick Kick

Your baby loves to follow directions. Say "kick kick" in rhythm to his feet. When he stops kicking, stop calling "kick kick!" The game will develop into a fun session of stop and go. Your baby is learning the enjoyment of language and at the same time exercising his muscles.

Quiet Time

Share a Book

Find opportunities every day to read a book with your baby. He will appreciate the closeness. Choose a sturdy book with familiar pictures. As you turn the pages, let your baby finger the pictures.

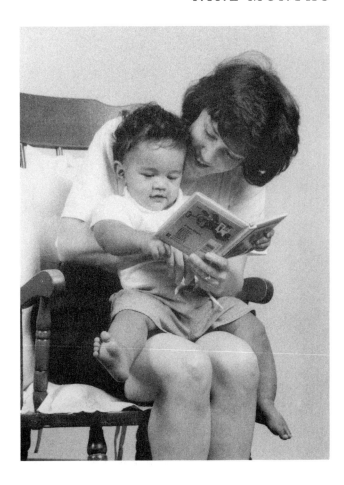

Sleep Waltz

Dance with your baby to quiet music before putting him to sleep. He has to spend much of his day exploring by himself on the floor. He needs some close cuddling before he falls asleep.

CHAPTER 11

TEN MONTHS

Baby's Viewpoint

Ten months is a perfect age for baby watching. Your ten-month-old is apt to be so busy with her own play agenda that she doesn't pay too much attention to her appreciative audience. At this age, she seems to be exploring a new question, "Can I use one object to make something happen to another object?" Of course, your baby asks this question with actions rather than words. Her experience playing with two objects at once has led naturally to the idea of using one object as a tool. Typical examples are using a spoon to chase a pea around her high chair tray, or using a strainer to bang out a tune on a pan.

As your baby becomes interested in more complicated social games, you will become aware of a change in your own way of playing, too. When your baby was under six months, the games you played most often involved back and forth conversations or exercises. Your baby enjoyed these contact games, which often were emotionally intense and laughter producing. As your baby learned to reach for and grasp toys, these play objects became prominent ingredients in parent-child play. Now that your baby is ten months old, contact games such as peek-a-boo, chase, and singing activities still provide a feeling of excitement and intimacy. However, new toy-playing and toy-sharing activities seem to predominate. Your baby is learning new things as she discovers new ways to play.

MOTOR SKILLS

At ten months of age, individual differences in motor development remain very apparent. While one ten-month-old baby might just be learning to creep, a second may already be a good walker. Despite the old adage, "You have to crawl before you walk," some babies spend little or no time in the crawling stage. They devote their energies to two-legged activities, pulling up on tables, chairs, or a parent's pant leg, and commanding their parents in a torrent of babbles to walk along holding their hands.

In marked contrast to the baby who is intent on walking is the baby who becomes an expert creeper. In actuality, a baby who is a proficient creeper gets around much more quickly, and is certainly better balanced, than the baby who is an early walker. She is also less likely to hurt herself when exploring new territory. Both the creeper and the walker can go around obstacles, climb up stairs, and investigate interesting objects.

A baby who is really into creeping will show a lengthy progression of skills, at first moving hands and legs one at a time, then developing a cross pattern creep with opposite hand and foot moving together, and finally creeping so quickly and smoothly that you will have difficulty identifying the pattern. The efficient creeper also learns to creep while holding an object or pushing a toy, much as the beginning walker tries to carry or push a toy.

Interestingly enough, there is no direct correlation between motor skills and intellectual ability. Knowing that a baby is an early walker tells us nothing about how bright that baby is, or whether she will be a good problem solver. Furthermore, independent walking cannot be rushed. Each baby has her own developmental timetable and will walk as soon as she is ready.

Most babies can pull themselves to a standing position at ten months of age. In fact, many babies will be steady enough to balance themselves without holding on. Your baby may take advantage of this new stability and use her hands to pound a table or low counter. In the morning, she may greet you by banging on the crib railing and crowing loudly. Later, you may see her standing at the coffee table, pounding on the top, and uttering a string of babbles. She is feeling very proud of her upright status.

Parents frequently ask whether playpens are a good idea for the ten-month-old baby. The answer is maybe. On the one hand, the ten-month-old baby is learning about space and objects, and being confined in a playpen would hamper her explorations. On the other hand, for babies who have just learned to pull up, the playpen is a safe place to practice. Also, playpens can be used to keep your baby safe and confined when you take her on an outing such as a picnic or a trip to the beach. If your baby is unhappy about staying in the playpen while in the house, get creative. Use the playpen to store toys, or take down one side of the playpen and let her crawl in and out.

When reaching and grasping, ten-month-olds can carry on tasks involving coordination of shoulder, arm, wrist, and fingers, such as taking the cover off a box or standing up a toy dog. If an object is placed in front of your baby, she reaches for it directly and picks it up deftly with forefinger and thumb. At an earlier age, she had to work hard to pick up a cereal-o. Now she can pick up a variety of small objects with a smooth and effortless grasp.

Now that your baby has mastered gripping with thumb and forefinger, she may be interested in tearing. The better she gets at tearing, the more fun she has. She can grasp the thin pages of a magazine or phone book and then rip them by rotating her wrist. Similarly, your baby may now be interested in stacking one small block on another. In order to accomplish this feat, your baby must lift a block up with her thumb and forefinger, place it on top of a second block, and then let go at just the right moment. If she succeeds, chances are that she will not rest on her laurels. Instead, she will place a third block on top of the second with the outcome, of course, the inevitable crash of the tower.

SEEING, HEARING, AND FEELING

An adult recognizes that, despite appearances, things do not get smaller as they move further away. We could hold a coffee cup in our hand and identify a same-sized coffee cup on the other side of the room. This ability to compensate for distance when we estimate size is called size constancy. Although some psychologists believe that infants have a built-in capacity to estimate size, it takes practice with space and objects before this capacity is fully developed. Your ten-month-old may provide clues that indicate she is acquiring a notion of size constancy. A large dog that she sees for the first time will frighten her, even when it is across the room, but she may be quite willing to play with a little dog that comes up to her.

Your baby's awareness of how things are supposed to look is demonstrated in many different ways. If you hand her a drinking cup upside down, she immediately turns it over. When her sister does a head stand, she watches her and laughs. She can also recognize a familiar object when she sees just a small part of it. She picks up a spoon almost covered by a napkin and puts it directly into her mouth.

With sounds as with sights, your baby's perceptions continue to sharpen. She's getting quite good at telling which direction a sound is coming from. If a sound is made behind her back, she turns around immediately and looks at the place it came from. She can easily recognize members of the family by voice alone, and can identify subtle differences in voice tone that show anger, teasing, calmness, joy, or annoyance.

At nine months old, your baby was especially interested in emptying out containers. At ten months, she is just as interested in how containers get filled up. She sticks her fingers into her own nose and ears, places rings on top of a spindle, and stuffs crackers into her mouth. The problem that your baby is most likely to be preoccupied with is what fits into what. She will use both hands and make grunting noises, for example, as she attempts to put a large measuring cup inside a smaller one. When her efforts to fit things together fail, she may hand both objects to an adult in a wordless request for assistance.

Your baby shows a new ability to solve problems involving the relationship of "behind" or "inside." If you hold a toy behind a clear plastic tray, she is likely to reach around the barrier to get the toy. A short time ago, she would have tried to retrieve it by reaching through the tray. You will see the same progression with a toy that is placed inside a clear container with a lid on it. Earlier your baby tried to get the toy by reaching either through the side or through the lid. Now she will push the lid off and reach inside to get her toy.

Another container skill that your baby may be interested in is dropping. At a younger age, when your baby dropped a toy, it was quite by accident. A few months later, your baby mastered the act of purposeful dropping. She was able to let go of one toy in order to take hold of another. Perhaps she enjoyed playing a game of dropping food and toys off her highchair. Now at ten months old, your baby is able to conduct deliberate experiments with dropping. She can hold her hand above a container, intentionally release a bunch of keys, and listen to the clatter as they hit the bottom of the pan.

KNOWING YOUR BABY

Your ten-month-old baby is usually friendly and outgoing. She uses her vocabulary of babbles to carry on a new conversation and enjoys experimenting with all kinds of new sound effects. She is becoming a good mimic and will try to copy sounds and words that are new to her. She has probably learned to understand several words and may show off her routines in front of a familiar audience. These routines may consist of word action games like, "Wave bye-bye to Auntie," "Throw Daddy a kiss," or "Play pat-a-cake with Nana."

The intense attachment to parents that characterizes the infant from six to nine months may show some signs of change. As creeping becomes easy and automatic and as your baby finds that she can get back to her starting point, she gets braver about leaving you behind as she explores. She now sees herself as a free agent, venturing across or out of the room and exploring new terrain. During her longer expeditions, she may take along a favorite blanket or toy. This toy or blanket becomes a security object that helps her to break old ties and gain independence.

When you and your baby are not on home territory there is a definite change in exploratory behavior. At first your baby restricts her play area to within touching distance of her parent. Even when she has worked up the courage to cross the room, your baby will check back to make sure that you stay put. You and your spouse provide your baby with a base of security that allows her to explore.

Some babies do not feel brave about exploring even when their parent is on the scene. If a new person enters the room your baby is likely to attach herself to a your leg and retain the leg hold until the visitor departs. When you are successful in getting away for a brief period, your baby may react to your return with a combination of clinging and angry behavior.

For babies who are reluctant to venture out, it is helpful to practice ways of saying good-bye. You can begin with a game of peek-a-boo in which you hide under a blanket. When your baby has learned to enjoy the peek-a-boo game, the next step is hiding in the room. At first you can reappear instantly with a happy, "Hi, Baby." After a while, wait a few seconds before you reappear. Once your baby is accustomed to disappearance acts in the room, try extending the game to outside of the room. A relative, a sibling, or a close friend can also be helpful in encouraging your baby's explorations. When your baby is left behind with someone she knows, it is much easier to say goodbye to a parent.

Having a substitute caregiver whom your baby loves and trusts is especially important for working parents. Many studies have been done on babies in child care with essentially the same outcome. If a baby is given loving care by a consistent caregiver, and receives quality care at home, the child-care experience is likely to be beneficial.

An at-home caregiver is an alternative to a child-care facility. Before hiring a new caregiver, check references very carefully. If possible, stay at home for the first day or so before leaving your baby with a new caregiver. Another possibility is to keep your baby at home with family child care, where a provider takes care of one to three babies in their home.

Your ten-month-old baby is able to predict what is going to happen in her home setting. In a new setting, she has no way of predicting what might happen next, and it's natural for her to feel less secure. If your baby has not been left with a substitute caregiver very often, you can anticipate that she will be fearful of a new child-care center or babysitter. Once you are assured that a substitute caregiver is competent and is interested in playing with your baby, be consistent and cheerful in the way you say goodbye. In time, your baby will establish a new set of predictions, and separation fears will resolve themselves.

Even when your baby has made a good adjustment to child care, she may fall apart when she comes home. Don't be surprised. Babies who have held it together all day with a caregiver may become cranky and clingy as soon as they see their parent. This doesn't mean your baby doesn't love you anymore. It means that your baby feels safe letting you know how she feels.

Even when your baby has become quite independent during the day, she may show signs of clinginess at night. She recognizes that being separated from you at night is not the same as being separated during the day. At night, she is stuck in the crib and there is no way to get to you. Parents solve this sleep time problem in different ways depending on their personal style. Some parents hold their baby until she falls asleep and then put her down in the crib. Some parents prefer to rely on bedtime routines, giving their baby a huggie, singing, patting, and giving last kisses until the baby allows them to leave. Some parents take their baby into their own bed. Still other parents do not want to get their baby in a habit they will not be able to break later. They put their baby in the crib cheerfully, but firmly, and endure the cries of distress as their baby settles down. There is no one right way for parents to solve this recurring sleep problem. Each family must search out an alternative that works well for them and their baby.

Suggested Activities

~~~~~~

SETTING THE STAGE

The ten-month-old is ready for variety. No matter how many interesting things there are to do inside, your baby really needs to have some outside time. A ride in the car, a walk outdoors, an excursion to the grocery store, a visit with a relative or playmate are important for parents and babies alike.

Your baby continues to enjoy structured playtime where you and your spouse set time aside just to play with your baby. In a two parent home, it is wise for each parent to play with their baby on a daily basis. Dads and Moms tend to have different play styles. Fathers are more likely to roughhouse and help their baby exercise. Mothers are more likely to focus on intellectual experiences. Both kinds of play provide important opportunities for development.

MAKING DISCOVERIES

Tube Talk

Disguise your voice by talking through a cardboard tube. You will be surprised at your baby's

attention. Now be silly. Make some sounds like "ba-ba-ba" or "ma-ma-ma!" Give a tube to your baby. Maybe she will imitate those sounds.

Baby Blocks

Make a series of red cardboard blocks and one yellow one. (Contact paper on pint size milk cartons works well.) Place a bell inside the yellow block. See if your baby prefers the yellow block.

Poke Box

Babies love to poke their fingers into tiny places. Here is an activity that utilizes this skill. Punch out two finger holes in the sides of a small, thin box. Line the box with different textures: fur, burlap, velvet, or sandpaper. Show your baby

how to poke her finger in a hole. (You can poke your finger in the other hole.) Discuss how it feels: soft, rough, bumpy. This is a great game to take in the car!

Seek and Find

Hide a clock or radio under a pillow. This will strengthen your baby's listening skills as she attempts to discover the clock.

Keeping Time

Make your baby a cereal box drum. Give her a wooden spoon to use as a drum stick. Encourage her to use it for banging.

Car Ride

Show your baby how to push a small car or truck along the floor. After a while, your baby will learn to let go so that the car rolls by itself.

Table Banging

Let your baby bang with both hands on a high chair or low table. Bring in another baby and see if they imitate each other.

Telephone Game

Talk to your baby on her play telephone, and then give her a turn. As your baby plays the telephone game, she learns the fun of carrying on a conversation. Unplugging a real phone works even better, but has some drawbacks. Your baby may want to return to her game when the phone has not been unplugged.

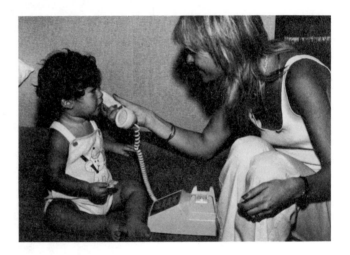

Magazine Tearing

Some babies at ten months are ready for tearing. Old magazines, tissue paper, wrapping paper, and foil provide interesting tearing experiences. Remember that your baby may also want to discover what the paper tastes like. Tearing activities require close supervision. If your baby is more interested in stuffing a wad of paper in her mouth than tearing it, reserve this activity for a later month.

MOTOR SKILLS

Sticks and Stones

> An outdoor yard provides your baby with an opportunity to practice putting things such as leaves, twigs, or toys in a pail. Make sure that your baby doesn't pick up a stone and put it in her mouth.

Follow the Leader

> This is an age when your baby loves to imitate. Play follow the leader with your baby, using simple gestures or hand play. Tap the table, open and close your fist, or put a hat on your head! Always talk about the things you are doing.

Spindle Toy

Make a spindle toy by inserting a cardboard tube from a toilet paper roll into the plastic top of a coffee can. Show your baby how to place a plastic bracelet over the spindle.

Reaching for Fun

If your baby is pulling up to a standing position, place some favorite toys on a low table so that your baby will have to stretch to reach them. This will give her practice in reaching and will increase her awareness of "close" and "far away."

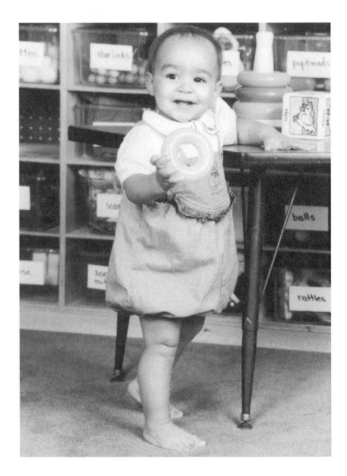

Paper Pull

Cut some contact paper into strips. Pull the backing off and stick it partly to a table. Start pulling the strip off: your baby will soon catch on. It's almost as much fun as peeling labels off of jars and bottles!

SOLVING PROBLEMS

Triple Feat

Give your baby a third toy when she has a toy in each hand. See if she can figure out how to hold all three toys.

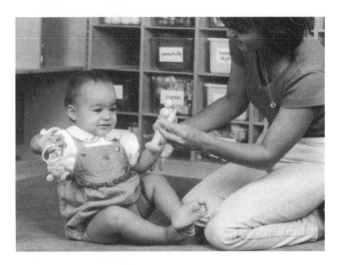

Shape Boxes

Cover three boxes—two square ones and one round one—with the same contact paper. Place cracker crumbs inside the round box. Will your baby discover that the round box holds the crackers?

Clothespin Drop

A handful of clothespins and a plastic bottle will help your baby learn how to fill and empty a container. She will need help at first, especially when it is time to empty the container. Later, vary the containers. An empty oatmeal container or coffee can will add to the fun!

Picture Hunt

When Daddy is away, it is fun to hide his picture. Where can he be? Under baby's dinner plate? Maybe in the toy box? In baby's shoe or even in his favorite book? Whenever it is discovered, shout, "Daddy!" Soon your baby will join in the fun! Other pictures can be substituted, but don't change too quickly or you will confuse your baby. Let Daddy play the game when Mommy is away.

Toy Hunt

Put a small toy inside a paper bag or box. As your baby struggles to get it out, she will increase her understanding of inside and outside.

Curler Play

Give your baby hair rollers of two different sizes. See if she is interested in placing one inside of the other.

Toy Tie

Tie a string onto the toys that your baby plays with in the highchair. Tie one end of the string to the highchair arm or tray. Trying to pull the toy back with the string will be a real challenge.

Where is Sister?

Show your baby two family photos (e.g. brother and sister). Cover both photos with a cloth. Ask your baby to find brother and then sister. You will be surprised at how much she understands.

DAILY ROUTINES

Mealtime

It All Stacks Up

All those empty kitchen containers—cereal boxes, cardboard juice containers, butter bowls, or egg cartons—make wonderful castles and bridges. Build a castle for your baby. She will enjoy watching them wobble and tumble.

Storehouse

Those kitchen building blocks need a place to live. Reserve a cabinet for your baby to house her mealtime games. Putting them away can be half the fun.

Sassy Seat

A sassy seat, which clamps to the table, makes mealtime more pleasant for a ten-month-old, especially if you go out to a restaurant. With a sassy seat, your baby can sit up at the table and will stay contented for a longer time. There are some disadvantages, of course. You can't feel safe with a tablecloth. Nor can you be sure that the food won't be tossed on the floor. (A plastic cloth spread out on the floor solves the cleanup problem.)

Restaurant Survival

If you do take your baby to a restaurant it's a good idea to take along a snack. Cracker bits, cheese bits, or unsweetened cold cereal in a paper bag works well. Even if the snack doesn't interest your baby, she will enjoy the challenge of reaching into the bag.

Bathtime

Bubble Blow

Your baby will enjoy blowing bubbles with a straw in her clean bath water. Blow through the straw and see if your baby will imitate you.

I Can Do It

Your baby is not too young to follow simple directions. She will be proud to wash her tummy or wash her toes!

Rain Rain

The bathtub is a good place to make rain. A small empty plastic container can easily be turned into a rain maker; just punch some holes in it with an ice pick. Let your baby fill it, then hold it up. Look out for the storm!

Washcloth Gifts

Wrapping a tub toy up in a washcloth adds a little mystery to your baby's bath. Encourage her to unwrap the wet cloth and discover her toy. She'll soon be wrapping up some gifts for you.

Quiet Time

Sand Man

Darken the room and turn on a flashlight. Move the light slowly around the room. Your baby will attempt to follow the light as it moves. Then, after a while, she may drop off to sleep.

Goodnight Music

Put a tape or CD on before your baby falls asleep. Turn down the volume as your baby closes her eyes.

CHAPTER 12

ELEVEN MONTHS

Baby's Viewpoint

In the last chapter, we talked about how the ten-month-old baby had learned the actions that go with certain standard phrases: "throw a kiss," "pat-a-cake," "how big is your baby?" Now we see your baby's understanding of language going beyond this vocabulary of action phrases. He attends to single words, and is beginning to recognize the names of familiar objects.

Now that your baby is interested in attaching meaning to single words, looking at pictures and reading books are likely to be favorite activities. Most babies show preferences for certain books. Cloth books, despite their advantages in terms of durability, are likely to be discarded. The pictures are just too dull. Books with glossy sturdy pages and very bright pictures, or books with interesting textures, are likely to be selected as favorites.

At first when your baby reads a book, he will play with it much as he plays with a toy, pulling at the pages, turning it in all directions, and throwing it on the floor. Only when these experiments are over will your baby be ready to focus on the contents.

Activity books, like *Pat the Bunny* or *Touch Me*, provide a good transition between a toy and a book. Your baby can look at the pictures, listen to the words, and, at the same time, pat a piece of cotton, poke his finger in a hole, or find a bunny hidden under a piece of fabric.

When your baby seems ready to enjoy a picture book, make sure to select a book with objects that are familiar to him. Some babies enjoy looking at books with large pictures: a telephone, a ball, a teddy bear, or a set of keys. Other babies like to find a picture of a particular character, such as Mickey Mouse, Winnie the Pooh, or Barney, who appears in different places on each page of the book.

Although parents quite naturally like to read a book to a baby while he is sitting on their lap, your baby may resist a position where he can't watch your face. Try sitting on the floor with your baby facing you and the book facing toward your baby. This way your baby can watch your face and the book at the same time.

MOTOR SKILLS

Although some eleven-month-old babies have mastered walking, most get from place to place by crawling on hands and knees. Babies who are eager to learn to walk may cruise along the furniture or insist on going on walks with their parents holding both hands. Balancing is the biggest challenge when babies first learn to walk. Typically, they will hold out their arms like wings, spread their legs, bend their knees, and lean forward as they toddle along. Parents with cameras or camcorders are likely to capture their babies first proud steps.

Another great accomplishment from the point of view of your baby is dropping, throwing, or hurling objects. Although parents are not delighted when their baby drops an ornament on the floor or flings his dish off the high chair, dropping, throwing, and flinging are important motor skills that your baby will practice and master.

SEEING, HEARING, AND FEELING

Your eleven-month-old baby enjoys new sights and sounds. A trip to the supermarket, for example, is an exciting experience. He will enjoy discovering the sound of a macaroni box when it is shaken, the feel of a banana, or the smell of a melon. Some babies are adventurous with new tastes. They may surprise you at their willingness to sample a mushroom or bite into a piece of cauliflower. Bring a nourishing snack from home—cheese, cereal-o's, or a favorite cracker— in case your baby becomes restless in the super- market.

Eleven-month-old babies are quite aware of differences in texture, and show decided prefer- ences. Some babies love the feel of sand between their toes, or the feel of wet and slippery things such as jello, yogurt, or ice cubes. Other babies are uncomfortable with any new tactile experi- ence. They don't like to play in a sandbox, walk barefoot on grass, finger-paint with whipped cream, or get a piece of tape stuck on their hands. If your baby is especially sensitive to dif- ferent feels, introduce new experiences gradu- ally, in a modified form. Put a little powder on the floor and let him touch it with his feet, or put a dab of yogurt on his index finger. As he experi- ences these more mild sensations, he will be less easily disturbed by differences in textures.

Because babies learn so much about their world through a sense of feel, a variety of experi- ences are important, even for babies who are sensitive to new sensations. Let your baby walk barefoot whenever possible. He will discover the coldness of bathroom tile, the roughness of car- peting, or the smoothness of wood. Contrary to popular belief, your baby does not need shoes for support when he first begins to walk.

By eleven months your baby has a good un- derstanding of spatial relationships like inside and behind. He knows when he is taking part in a hide-the-toy game, and he is much harder to fool. At a younger age when you moved a toy from one hiding place to another, he searched for it in the place where you hid it the first time. Now, he watches your hand carefully and likes to go to the second hiding place.

Placing one object inside another can still be a difficult task. Given two measuring cups that differ in size, your baby decides which cup fits into the other on a trial and error basis. The larger cup may be banged against the smaller with a real show of strength before your baby is convinced that it will not fit inside.

Placing small objects in a larger container presents an easier challenge and may turn into a virtual obsession. Over and over again, your baby will drop items into the container, take them out and then drop them in again. A parent watching the activity will lose interest long before the infant, who repeats the task with obvious purpose and enjoyment.

KNOWING YOUR BABY

Your baby's ability to communicate leaps forward between ten and twelve months old. At a younger age his major communications were associated with feelings. In a variety of ways, your baby told you when he was feeling happy or sad, silly or whiny, restless or contented. During the last quarter of the first year, your baby is able to communicate some very specific messages. Parents who are with their baby all the time may not be as aware as outsiders of these changes in baby's communication skills. Often parents get the best descriptions of new language events from a visiting friend or grandparent. Here are some typical reports from proud and observant grandmothers.

"Rosemary is so smart, you won't believe it. I took her in the swimming pool, and she loved it. When I brought her inside to dress her, I had her standing by the window. She looked outside, saw the pool, and got all excited. She pulled at the neck of her romper suit, pointed to the pool, and made these really urgent 'oh-oh' sounds. She was really trying to let me know that she wanted to go back in the pool."

"I know you think I'm exaggerating, but Nicholas is really beginning to talk. He says 'ha ba' when he wants to play ball, 'da da' when he sees a dog, and 'mmm' when he sees his supper coming. And when I read him the Three Bears story and showed him the page where Goldilocks eats the porridge, Nicholas said 'mmm.' I think he was telling me that he wanted to have some cereal."

In addition to communicating with meaningful sounds, your baby is interested in the names of objects. On a trip to the grocery store, he will pay attention when you name the names of the foods on the shelves, such as milk, bananas, bread, or cereal. On a car ride, point out familiar objects such as a bus, dog, or airplane. He will also pay attention to phrases in a song like "pop goes the weasel" or "all fall down." Although your baby will not always perform on cue, you will continue to see growth in his understanding of language.

In addition to tuning into language, your baby is probably showing a special interest in people. By now, he has made friends with quite a few different adults. Though these adults cannot compete with Mom and Dad, familiar adults are honored with a special greeting. A common way for your baby to acknowledge familiar adults is to offer them a toy.

When he discovers that adults are fun to play with, he will insist on being where the action is. If family and friends are sitting at the table, he wants to be there, too. If a passenger rides in the front seat of the car, he will object to staying in the back seat. A sassy seat is a good way to bring baby up to the table if he wants to join the party. The car problem is more difficult to deal with. It may help to have everyone in the car sing a song together. Never succumb to the temptation of bringing your baby to the front seat.

Although increased social skills for most babies make it easier to leave them with a sitter, or in a child-care setting, your baby may be clingier than he was at eight months. You may find that your baby is on constant vigil, making sure that you don't slip out of his sight. Eventually this behavior passes and your baby will become more comfortable about your leaving, as he realizes that you always come back. In the last chapter, we talked about sleep problems that appear toward the end of the first year. Sleep problems are likely to be cyclical. Just as you feel secure about getting a full night's sleep, your baby may revert to waking every few hours.

If your baby will not sleep through the night, and a diaper change or a drink does nothing to calm him down, you may want to solve the problem by putting your baby into your bed. On the other hand, you may not be willing to establish a pattern that is difficult to change. Another solution is to stay in your baby's room and rock, pat, or sing him back to sleep.

Suggested Activities

~~~~~~

SETTING THE STAGE

The eleven-month-old is ready for new experiences: seeing new sights, making new friends, and visiting new places. You will be amazed at how much your baby understands, and how well he follows simple directions. He searches for a ball that has disappeared under the sofa, and pulls a ribbon to recapture a toy. He is pleased with his newfound ability to push, pull, and climb, and will practice these skills at every opportunity. Baby-proofing your home is an absolute must! Your baby will be quite adept at pulling on lamp cords, pushing plants off tables, and climbing on new white chairs. He will keep you on your toes, and it will be more difficult than ever to find a relaxing moment. At the same time, every minute with your baby will be full of fun and surprises.

EXPLORING NEW HORIZONS

Car Rides

Your baby enjoys a car ride but will not fall asleep in the car as quickly as he did at a younger age. String large beads or hair rollers across his car seat to help him enjoy the ride.

New Adult Friends

Although your baby may still not want you out of sight, he enjoys making new adult friends as long as he makes the overtures. Your baby will warm up faster to new people if they start off by offering him a toy.

Restaurant Challenges

Parents as well as babies enjoy an occasional meal out. Unfortunately, your baby at eleven months may be in the throwing-food stage and taking him to a restaurant may present problems. Possible solutions include bringing along a sassy seat so that your baby can sit right up at the table, bringing along a bag of toys or nutritious snack foods that will capture your baby's interest, or choosing a fast food restaurant that is set up for food-throwing babies.

LEARNING TO COMMUNICATE

Feed the Puppet

Put your hand inside an animal hand puppet. Give your baby a ball. Ask your baby to feed the puppet. After a couple of demonstrations, your baby may understand your words.

Little Daddy

Give your baby a comb and a baby doll. See if he will comb the doll's hair.

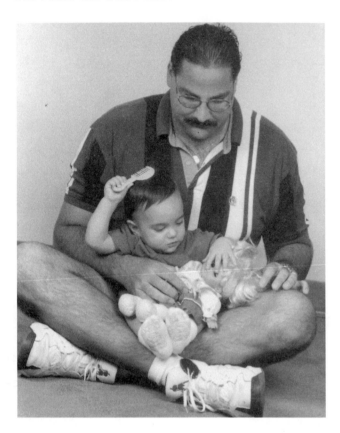

Out the Window

When you hear an airplane or a bird, take your baby to the window and talk about what you see.

Getting a Laugh

Your eleven-month-old is developing a sense of humor and will laugh at an incongruous event. Pretend to drink from his bottle or put on his shoe. Change the game: Let your baby put on your shoe.

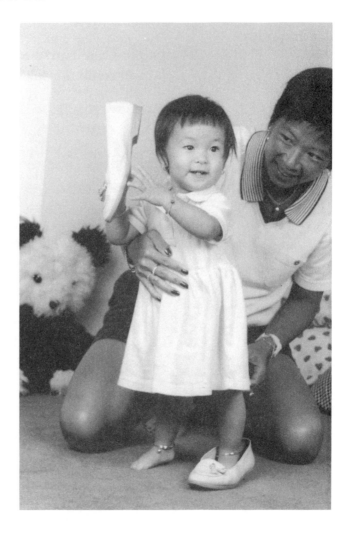

MAKING DISCOVERIES

Spoon Rhythms

Let your baby beat out rhythms with a wooden spoon on the back of a muffin pan or a pie plate.

Tunnel Play

Roll a toy car through a cardboard tube. See if your baby will watch for it to come out the other end.

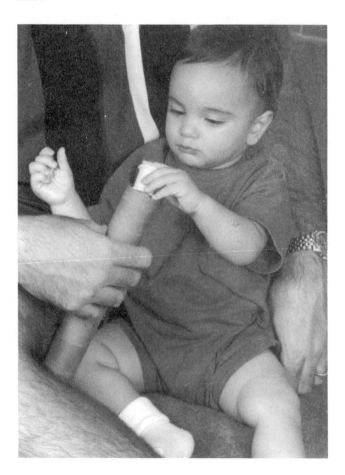

Ribbon Pull

Tie a ribbon on one or two of your baby's toys. Let your baby watch as you hide the toys under the sofa. See if your baby will pull the ribbons to retrieve his toys.

Lever Play

Your baby is learning how to push down a lever. Let him practice with a musical top.

MOTOR SKILLS

Chair Walkers

If your baby is walking, show him how to hold onto a child-sized chair and push it around the room.

Sticky Stuff

Pull the back off a large piece of contact paper. Tape it on the floor with the sticky side up. Let your baby walk across it. He may have fun trying to escape from it.

Stroller Push

If your baby is an early walker, let him push his own stroller. It's a great balance exercise and gives him practice with starting and stopping. A light stroller will be more stable if you weigh it down with a heavy book.

Underfoot

Whether your baby is walking on his own or holding onto your hand, he will enjoy the experience of walking on different surfaces. Give him a chance to walk barefoot on a carpet, floor, or take him to the beach and let him walk on the sand.

SOLVING PROBLEMS

Zipper Baby

Dress a doll or bear in an outfit with a zipper. Show your baby how the zipper goes up and down. Before long, he will try to pull down the zipper.

Mitt Play

Give your baby an oven mitt. By trial and error your baby will discover how to put his hand inside the mitt. He may carry out an experiment and put the mitt on his foot.

Film Can Fun

Place bits of crackers or cereal inside a small, screw-top film container or plastic jar. Place the lid top on loosely (do not turn). Show your baby how to take off the lid and retrieve the crumbs.

Ball Rolling Games

Roll a ball to your baby and encourage him to roll it back. Chant a song as you play the game.

We roll the ball, it's rolling,
Now roll it down the track.
We roll it down to Baby,
And Baby rolls it back.

Wrap-Up Toy

Wrap up a toy in tissue paper and let your baby unwrap it. If you choose a toy that your baby stopped playing with, finding it in the tissue may renew your baby's interest.

Tote Bag

Make your baby a flannel tote bag to wear over his shoulder. Let him reach inside and get different toys.

Pet Play

If you are planning to get a puppy or a kitten for your baby, this is a good age to do it. Your baby is not strong enough to hurt the pet and will enjoy playing with it. When your baby gets older and plays more roughly, the pet will be bigger too, and will be able to protect himself.

Stand-Up Toys

Give your baby a stuffed animal that sits up. Place the animal on its side and see if your baby will place it back in a sitting position.

DAILY ROUTINES

Mealtime

Cereal Pour

Paper cups and cereal-o's make good pouring tools. They are not as messy as water but achieve the same results. Fill a cup with cereal-o's. Show your baby how to pour them into another cup—then another cup. He will enjoy sampling the cereal-o's.

Flour Paint

Writing is magic when we use flour instead of pencil. Spread a thin layer of flour on a clean smooth surface. Demonstrate how to rub your finger in the flour and make circles, zig zags, and slashes.

Cup and Spoon

A paper cup and a tablespoon will challenge your baby's filling ability. Show him how to dip the spoon in a bowl of water and pour some water in the cup. Small bits of ice will add to the interest and the challenge.

Bathtime

Duck Soup

Water play is always a valuable experience for your baby. Give your baby a soup strainer and ladle. Place some small floating ducks in the tub. When your baby is in the tub, he may try to catch the duck in the strainer.

Wall Washing

Give your baby a sponge and let him clean the tub. He will enjoy making circles and up and down strokes.

Diaper time

Sticker Fun

The difficult time of diapering becomes a little easier if you let your baby decorate a diaper with stickers. He'll enjoy putting them on the new diaper and you'll be glad to get that clean diaper in place.

Diapering Teddy

Make a small cloth diaper for a small teddy bear. Sew Velcro tabs on each side. Let your baby watch as you put the diaper on his teddy bear. It will make diaper time more fun.

Tape and Tape

When your baby is especially wiggly on the changing table, sometimes a piece of scotch tape is a good distracter. The fun of putting it on and taking it off will last at least as long as it takes to diaper your baby.

Quiet Time

Squeaking Pictures

Make or buy your baby a squeaking picture book and "read" the book with your baby at bedtime. As you turn the pages, let your baby make the pictures squeak. Squeaks can be bought at novelty stores and glued or sewed under pieces of fabric in homemade picture books.

Sleep Song

Choose a favorite lullaby and sing it to your baby at night as he falls asleep. If your baby hears the same lullaby every night, he will relax and fall asleep when he hears you sing.

CHAPTER 13

TWELVE MONTHS

Baby's Viewpoint

The picture of baby on her first birthday with both hands plunged into the cake is a favorite photo in many family albums. Your twelve-month-old is very busy exploring. From the moment of birth she has been actively taking in information about her environment. In the beginning months, her explorations were limited to searching with her eyes, listening to sounds, and identifying new sensations. From three to six months, her explorations were extended as she reached out with her hands, manipulated objects, and playfully fingered her parent's face. During the second half of the first year, your baby learned to crawl, creep, and pull to a standing position, and her field of exploration expanded.

As your baby launches into her second year of life, you will notice a subtle difference in the way she explores her environment. Her active explorations are turning into experiments. She is not only interested in dumping out the contents of Mother's purse, she is looking for new ways to accomplish it. She may start off on the floor beside the purse, pulling out objects one at a time. Pretty soon she sticks both hands into the purse and scoops out the contents. As a final maneuver, she stands up, purse in hand, turns it over, and watches the contents spill out over the floor.

The same kind of experimentation that we see going on with objects is even more striking with people. Your baby is becoming aware of her ability to create a reaction and, during a social exchange, she is likely to play to her audience. A few months ago, she would hand an object to a visitor and take it back again in a kind of social game. Now, we can see an element of teasing creeping into her back and forth games. Your baby will spontaneously offer a cookie to a visitor. As soon as the visitor goes to bite the cookie, she whisks it away and smiles impishly. Her intent to tease is unmistakable.

This increased awareness of people's behavior is also evident in your baby's imitation skills. Now your baby imitates, not only the actions you model, but actions that you are unaware of. She may wipe her high chair tray after a spill, or mimic adults who are absentmindedly tapping their fingers or pulling on an ear lobe. She will especially enjoy making faces and will copy a scowl or a crinkled up nose.

Your twelve-month-old's increased proficiency in imitation is coupled with a leap forward in language development. She jabbers with expression as she plays with her toys, follows directions like "touch your nose," and is acquiring her own words, such as "mo" for more and "na-na" for grandmother or banana. If you watch closely, you may even see the early emergence of pretend play.

At first, the pretend play of your baby is highly imitative, but it gives us a glimpse of what is to come. After watching you, she will hold her doll in her arms and give it a vigorous hug when it falls to the floor. A little later, she hugs the doll spontaneously. At another time, she may push a toy car along the floor, making "vrum-vrum" noises. Her ability to replay a familiar scene or experience signals an important developmental advance. You will have many opportunities to encourage this development in the months ahead.

MOTOR SKILLS

At one year, most babies have become quite adept at getting around the house, even if they haven't learned to walk. Babies seem interested not only in what is in front of them or behind them, but also in things that are out of reach. Many babies climb on anything they can pull themselves up on. They are never as good, however, at getting down from things as they are at getting up. As your baby becomes more adept at climbing up on things, she may become increasingly fearful about getting down. This is not a regression. It is a new respect for high places and a new awareness of danger.

Bathtime offers a good opportunity to observe your baby's developing motor skills. Your baby is not only splashing with her hands, but her feet too may get into the act. She may also try standing up in the bath, or even climbing out. No-skid strips on the bottom of the tub makes bathtime a little safer.

Although your baby may have just mastered the art of walking, she may already be combining her walking with other skills. She may walk and pull, walk and push, or walk and carry toys at the same time. If there is an older sibling around to imitate, she may even try some gymnastics. She will put her head on the floor in a mock somersault, and then look around for applause.

Throwing is another motor skill your baby is practicing. Sometimes she throws for the sheer joy of it. At other times she is especially interested in where the toy is going. She may gently throw a ball to Daddy two or three times and then try a bigger throw in a different direction. With rapt attention, she watches the ball bounce off the wall or down the steps.

If the climate permits, swimming is a delightful activity for your baby. Most babies feel quite comfortable about putting their head in the water, and a back and forth swim between Mom and Dad is a favorite activity. Some babies enjoy a swim tube seat where they can glide across the pool and splash with their hands. Swim rings should not be used for the one-year-old because it is much too easy to slip through the hole.

Enrolling your baby in a swimming class may increase your baby's skills, although it is very unlikely that she will become a true swimmer. The principle benefits of any early swimming program is that it can help babies feel more relaxed in the water. If your baby is frightened by formal lessons, even when you are with her, she is letting you know that she isn't ready.

SEEING, HEARING, AND FEELING

Your baby loves to experiment with new sensations: wet slimy jello, sticky icing, or hard cold ice cubes. Keeping her hands out of her food during mealtime is just about impossible. She splashes the oatmeal, smears the apple juice, and dips her fingers into the orange juice. Even the most finicky parents abandon their struggle to keep their baby clean.

Differences in sounds are just as interesting to your baby as differences in texture. She will tap a spoon against a glass, a plate, a bowl, or her high chair. She tries different vocalizations such as a shout, a string of jabbers that sounds like talking, or a kind of sing-song. She may awaken in the morning and practice her jabbers for a good twenty minutes before calling out for attention.

Your baby's scientific experiments and investigations are probably most apparent when she is playing with objects. Favorite activities now include stirring with a spoon, inverting a container to pour out the contents, or pulling a toy by a string. All these investigations have in common the fact that your baby, on a primitive level, is learning to use a tool.

Your baby's ability to experiment is fortified by a new level of strength and a new determination to find out if things come apart. Instead of playing with the suction toy on her high chair, she will pull and push at it until it finally comes off. Your baby tries harder than ever to make objects go back together again, to get the blocks back into the shape sorter, or to reconnect a set of pop beads.

Although your one-year-old may sometimes feel frustrated when objects won't do her bidding, her repertoire of accomplishments is growing. She may be able to transfer a spoonful of food, hold on to a cup, or open a small box of raisins. She is probably learning how to scoop up water with a bath toy, pull a shoelace until it unties, pick a leaf off a plant, slip a necklace over her head, scribble with a pencil, and open up a cabinet by pulling on the knob.

KNOWING YOUR BABY

By the time they are a year old, some babies have mastered their first word, and will use it on every possible occasion. This word is really more than just a word. It represents a whole sentence. "Mommy" may mean, "Mommy, come in and get me." "Ba-ba" may mean, "I want my bottle right now!" Even if your baby is not using words, she may understand language quite well. She may know the names of everyone in the family and look toward the person whose name is called. She may even point out pictures of family members in a photograph album. And when you tell her to "Wave Daddy goodbye," your baby's response is quite different from her response to "Daddy's coming home." Some parents actually resort to spelling, instead of saying "bedtime" or "going out."

As your baby's ability to understand language grows, she will learn to follow simple directions. Typically babies learn the meaning of one or two common phrases, like "Give me," "Show me," and "Where is." Once your baby has learned these key phrases, she will learn to follow several different commands like "Show me

your eyes," "Show me your belly button," "Show me your toys," or "Get Mommy's keys."

Although babies are delighted with their ability to follow directions, your one-year-old may also know how to tease. When you ask her to hand you something, she may start to go for it, but then bring you something else. The fact that she is watching your reaction and smiling broadly suggests that it is all in fun.

Along with the ability to tease adults comes an awareness of the meaning of "no." At ten months old, "no" to your baby meant stop for a second and then go ahead. Now, at twelve months, "no" really stands for a prohibition. When a parent says "no" to a twelve-month-old, a common reaction is a show of temper, or a shower of tears.

Your baby's readiness to try out new things extends to the social realm. She is delighted with the opportunity to play with other children. With older children, especially siblings, your baby will watch for a while to see what toys the children are playing with. She will then devote all her efforts to getting her hands on those toys.

When your one-year-old plays with another child, the play is likely to progress from watching to mimicking each other. Peers who know each other well may offer a toy to a friend, or monitor their friend's expression when they take the toy away. During the next year, beginning with momentary exchanges and progressing to hour long intervals, your baby will learn the joy of playing with another child.

Playfulness, curiosity, a readiness to experiment—these are qualities that make your one-year-old a delightful companion. As you and your baby play together during the second year, you will become more and more aware of the ways in which she is developing as a unique and separate person. At times she will tease and defy you. At times she will use you as a resource. At times she will proudly share her new discoveries, and at times she will come to you for comfort and affection.

The second year of life will provide you and your baby with new challenges, and new opportunities to learn and grow. The time you have spent with your baby during the first year, the games that you have played, and the love you have shared have prepared you to meet the challenges and reap the benefits of your baby's second year.

Suggested Activities

SETTING THE STAGE

Your twelve-month-old is an active experimenter who needs time by herself to carry on her constant investigations. Make your baby's environment fun to explore. Place cartons with interesting things inside them around the room. Hide a toy behind a chair, or tie short ribbons onto toys so that your baby can pull them.

Your baby will make all sorts of new discoveries. Talk to your baby about things that capture her interest: a shadow on the wall, a crinkling sound, a smooth, warm stone. The more enthusiasm you show, the more she is encouraged to explore and investigate.

MAKING DISCOVERIES

Sandbox Play

A soup strainer is a good toy for the sandbox. It is easy for your baby to manipulate, and she will experiment with holding it at different heights as she watches the sand pour out.

Car Roll

Fold a piece of cardboard to make a hill. Show your baby how to place the car on top of the hill and let it roll down.

Junk Toy

Stringing odd rattles, toys, and containers on a cord makes a silly and wonderful pull toy. Soon your baby will bring you things to add to her toy.

Stacking Blocks

Large cardboard nesting alphabet blocks make a wonderful first birthday present. They can be used in a variety of ways—as containers, as building blocks, and as a nesting toy.

Scribbling

The high chair is an ideal spot to practice scribbling. Because your baby is more interested in manipulating the crayon than producing a work of art, let her practice on scrap paper or a large thrown-away envelope.

Music Lover

Twelve months is an ideal time to help your baby become an eclectic music lover. When you ride in the car with your baby, play a variety of music selections, including some of the classics. Babies who are introduced to fine music at an early age develop a love for music that is likely to be sustained. And some studies have shown that listening to classical music helps a baby acquire spatial reasoning. Because spatial reasoning is an important mathematical skill, children who have been exposed to classical music are likely to do better in math.

MOTOR SKILLS

Raking Game

Show your baby how to use a small mop to gather out-of-reach toys. Make sure that you play this game while your baby is sitting down. Letting her walk around with a stick is not a good idea.

Shadow Play

Take your baby out on a sunny day and show her shadows. Stand on her shadow and let her stand on yours.

Bean Bag Toss

Give your baby a bean bag and a large sand pail. Show her how to toss the bean bag into the pail.

Big Ball Play

Roll a beach ball or large plastic ball down a slight incline, or toss it against the wall. Your baby will have a good time chasing it.

Stepping High

If your baby is walking now, put a row of blocks in front of her and let her step over it. This will give her practice in maintaining her balance.

Tunnel Game

Make a tunnel by spreading your legs and let your baby walk through. She will enjoy this special game of peek-a-boo.

Ribbon Pull

If your baby is walking, tie a ribbon on to a stuffed animal and send her off on a pet walk.

Sit-on Toy

Babies who have mastered walking may be ready for a sit-on push toy. Make sure that the one you buy is stable and low enough for your baby to get on and off by herself.

Clothespin Game

Show your baby how to slip old-fashioned clothespins around the rim of a plastic container.

Mini Chair

Babies who have learned to walk enjoy the challenge of sitting by themselves in a small chair. Look for a sturdy canvas or cushioned chair that is wide enough for your baby to climb in front-wards and then turn around. In the beginning babies have difficulty backing into chairs.

SOLVING PROBLEMS

Shoe Find

Put out several pairs of shoes and place them on the floor in front of your baby. Pick up one shoe and give it to your baby. See if she can find its match.

Block Tower

Build a block tower out of alphabet blocks. Give your baby a turn. Don't be surprised if your baby would rather knock down your tower than build one of her own.

Magic Cups

Your baby will enjoy activities that provide a challenge. Place two cups in front of her. Next, put a small toy under one cup. Ask your baby, "Where is the toy?" Lift the cup to show her where it is. Do this several times. Does your baby find the toy without your help?

Color Spools

Give your baby a container with a lid, several regular-size spools painted blue, and one giant-size spool painted red. Make a hole in the lid big enough for the regular-size blue spool but too small for the red spool. Your baby will discover which spools fit in the hole.

Push Car

Give your baby a toy car. See if she can push it along the floor. Tie a string to the car. Now is she able to pull it?

Tunnel Play

Make a tunnel out of a cereal box. Show your baby how to push a car through the tunnel. She will watch for the car to come out at the other end.

Tube Play

Give your baby a long cardboard tube from the center of a gift wrapping roll. Show her how the tube can be used to push a ball along the floor.

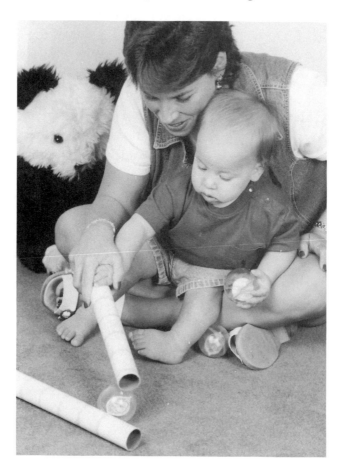

Cups and Saucers

Put two plastic cups and two plastic saucers in front of your baby and let her play. She may turn the cups upside down, pile them up, or put a cup in each saucer.

LANGUAGE AND IMITATION

Naming Games

Put a few items in a shoe box, such as a spoon, a toy car, and a cup. Name each item as your baby pulls it out of the box. The more you play naming games with your baby, the more opportunities she has to learn language.

Older Friends

If your baby doesn't have siblings, invite some older children over to play. Your baby will attempt to mimic what they are doing and you will be surprised how many new things she learns.

Mommy's Helper

Give your baby a sponge so that she can help wipe her own high chair.

Playing Parent

Give your baby a stroller or shopping cart and send her for a stroll with her doll. Pretending and language development go together.

Purse Play

Give your baby an old wallet, some keys and a purse. Your baby will feel important carrying around these grown up possessions. At the same time, your baby will attempt to open the purse, place the wallet inside the purse, or place the key in a keyhole.

Doll Bath

Put a large baby doll in the bath with your baby. Wash the baby doll's hair. Now let your baby have a turn.

Dancing Lesson

By twelve months old your baby is ready for a home-style dancing lesson. Hold your baby's hands and let her bop up and down in time with a lively tune, or hold her in your arms as you dance to a favorite tape.

Clapping Fun

If your twelve-month-old has mastered clapping, put on a marching tape and clap to the music with your baby.

Family Album

Make your baby her own family album. Be sure to include her favorite people and her favorite pets.

Reading Time

Read to your baby. See if she would like to turn the pages by herself.

First Birthday Scrap Book

Save cards, invitations, and ribbons from your baby's first party and put them in an album along with a sequence of birthday party photos. When your baby is older, she will enjoy looking back at pictures of her first birthday.

A Closing Thought

This book includes a variety of games and play ideas. Perhaps you have noticed that some of the suggested activities are repeated in different months. This kind of repetition is important for infants. Revisiting an old experience can provide a new opportunity to learn as your baby brings new capabilities into the learning situation.

Remember, too, that even at a very young age your baby will enjoy the company of another baby. Invite a couple over with their baby. As you try out the activities together, you will double the fun of baby watching.

You are your baby's first teacher, but in a manner of speaking, your baby is your teacher, too. Every baby is a unique personality, making an indelible impression on the people who are caring for him, enriching their lives in countless and subtle ways. As you watch your baby grow and learn in these early months of life, you, his parents, share in the learning experience.

Index

~~~~~~

About the Author

MARILYN SEGAL, PH.D., a developmental psychologist specializing in early childhood, is professor of human development and director of the Family Center at Nova Southeastern University in Fort Lauderdale, Florida. The mother of five children, she has written thirteen previous books, including *Making Friends* and *Just Pretending*. She is also the creator of the nine-part television series "To Reach a Child."

PARENTING/CHILDCARE BOOKS FROM NEWMARKET PRESS

Ask for these titles at your local bookstore or use this coupon and enclose a check or money order payable to: **Newmarket Press**, 18 E. 48th St., NY, NY 10017.

Baby Massage
____ $11.95 pb (1-55704-022-2)
How to Help Your Child Overcome Your Divorce
____ $14.95 pb (1-55704-329-9)
How Do We Tell the Children?
____ $18.95 hc (1-55704-189-X)
____ $11.95 pb (1-55704-181-4)
Inner Beauty, Inner Light: Yoga for Pregnant Women
____ $18.95 pb (1-55704-315-9)
In Time and With Love
____ $21.95 hc (0-937858-95-1)
____ $12.95 pb (0-937858-96-X)
Loving Hands: Traditional Baby Massage
____ $15.95 pb (1-55704-314-0)
Mothering the New Mother, Rev. Ed.
____ $16.95 pb (1-55704-317-5)
My Body, My Self for Boys
____ $11.95 pb (1-55704-230-6)
My Body, My Self for Girls
____ $11.95 pb (1-55704-150-4)
My Feelings, My Self
____ $11.95 pb (1-55704-157-1)
Raising Your Jewish/Christian Child
____ $12.95 pb (1-55704-059-1)
The Ready-to-Read, Ready-to-Count Handbook
____ $11.95 pb (1-55704-093-1)

Saying No Is Not Enough, Rev. Ed.
____ $14.95 pb (1-55704-318-3)
The Totally Awesome Business Book for Kids (and Their Parents)
____ $10.95 pb (1-55704-226-8)
The Totally Awesome Money Book for Kids (and Their Parents)
____ $18.95 hc (1-55704-183-0)
____ $10.95 pb (1-55704-176-8)
The What's Happening to My Body? Book for Boys
____$18.95 hc (1-55704-002-8)
____$11.95 pb (0-937858-99-4)
The What's Happening to My Body? Book for Girls
____ $18.95 hc (1-55704-001-X)
____ $11.95 pb (0-937858-98-6)
Your Child at Play: Birth to One Year, Rev.
____ $24.95 hc (1-55704-334-5)
____ $15.95 pb (1-55704-330-2)
Your Child at Play: One to Two Years, Rev.
____ $24.95 hc (1-55704-335-3)
____ $15.95 pb (1-55704-331-0)
Your Child at Play: Two to Three Years, Rev.
____ $24.95 hc (1-55704-336-15)
____ $15.95 pb (1-55704-332-9)
Your Child at Play: Three to Five Years, Rev.
____ $24.95 hc (1-55704-337-X)
____ $15.95 pb (1-55704-333-7)

For postage and handling, please add $3.00 for the first book, plus $1.00 for each additional book. Prices and availability are subject to change.

I enclose a check or money order payable to **Newmarket Press** in the amount of _____

Name _____

Address _____

City/State/Zip _____

For discounts on orders of five or more copies or to get a catalog,
contact Newmarket Press, Special Sales Department, 18 East 48th Street, NY, NY 10017;
Tel.: 212-832-3575 or 800-669-3903; Fax: 212-832-3629.

MAC:\projects\ads\bob's\YCAP1bob.qxd 6/10/98